Grove and Gallows

Grove and Gallows
Greek and Latin Sources
For Germanic Heathenism

James Chisholm

2002

First Edition, June 2002

Second Edition Published by
Runestar
P.O. Box 16
Bastrop, Texas 78602

2018

runa@texas.net

Acknowledgements

Thanks to Edred Thorsson for proposing this project back in 1985, and for publishing the first version in 1987. Thanks also to my brother Gary for computer help. Thanks to Dianne Ross and Mike Rigby for proofreading and critical advice.

By Hercules, the man was greater than Caesar or Cromwell—nay, nearly equal to Odin and Thor. The Texans ought to build him an altar."

Thomas Carlyle, on hearing of Bowie's death at the Alamo.

Spirits of the mighty, though fallen! Honors and rest are with ye: the spark of immortality which animated your form shall brighten into flame, and Texas, the whole world, shall hail ye like the demigods of old, as founders of new actions, and as patterns of imitation.

Telegraph and Texas Register, March 24, 1836

i

TABLE OF CONTENTS

INTRODUCTION

This is a collection of the most significant Latin and Greek literary sources concerning pre-Christian Germanic religion up to the 12th century A.D. None of these sources were written by practitioners of pre-christian Germanic religion. The sources generally reflect the attitudes of either pagan Romans or christianized Romans or christianized Germanic peoples. Although various Germanic peoples inhabited parts of France, Spain and Italy during the late Roman and early Medieval periods, it is often difficult to tell whether many Christian descriptions of paganism in these areas refer to Germanic, Roman, Celtic practices. Unless it reasonably clear that a source refers to a practice among Germanic peoples it has not been included here.

PURPOSE

This assembly of literary sources for traditional Germanic religious practices should be supplemented by a study of archaeological sources. Grove and Gallows is useful as a platform for your own researches, or may be profitably used in conjunction with general descriptions of Germanic religion and culture which often cite these sources but do not quote them in full, if at all.

HOW TO USE THIS BOOK

You do not need to read this section unless this book's organization is not intuitively clear to you.

These sources have been arranged chronologically. In the main heading you will either find the name of an author or the title of the work if the author's identity is not known. You will find short descriptions of the author and or the passage's subject matter under the main heading. The author's works are then subdivided beneath the main subheadings. You will generally find two levels of subheadings. The first level of subheading contains the work's title, if any. If you were looking at Caesar's Gallic War, you would find 'Julius Caesar' in the main heading and Gallic War as the first level of subheading. In the third level of subheading you will find topic headings that give you a general idea as to the contents of a given passage. All three heading levels are included in the table of contents. For example:

JULIUS CAESAR (main heading)

Julius Caesar lived between 100 and 44 B.C.E. He began climbing the Roman 'ladder of honors' as a prosecutor in 78 B.C.E. and kept on climbing until he was elected Consul in 59 B.C.E. He conquered Gaul between 58 and 50 B.C.E. During his Gallic campaigns, Caesar dealt with Germanic tribes and wrote about them in his <u>Gallic War</u>, which he wrote around 52-51 B.C.E. to further his political career. A short section of the <u>Gallic War</u> is devoted to Germanic anthropology.

<u>GALLIC WAR</u> (main subheading)

New Moon (secondary subheading)

In this case we know the name of the passage's author, so his name, Julius Caesar, appears at the top as the main heading. If we would not have known the author of this passage, we would have put the book's title, *Gallic War,* in the main heading. The italicized paragraph beneath the main heading provides background information about Julius Caesar and the gallic wars. The underlined and capitalized heading beneath the introductory text is where you will find the book's title in cases where we know the author's name. If we know the author's name, we go straight to the third level heading. The italicized heading beneath describes the general nature of the passage or some hopefully memorable idea that you can associate with the passage. These third level headings are not given by the authors and not a part of the original texts. I included them to make this book more user friendly.

If you want to research a particular topic, such as sacred groves, you can use the index to find all the references to the term grove, wood, trees etc. You may then write these down and go to each page listed in the index for these topics. Then sort out the passages that treat the topic you are researching. This may then be combined with whatever data you pull from the other medieval sources, such as those in Old English and Old Norse. Those sources have not been conveniently collected under a single cover, so you will have to spend more time in the libraries to get a complete picture.

THE TEXTS

JULIUS CAESAR

Julius Caesar lived between 100 and 44 B.C.E. He began climbing the Roman 'ladder of honors' as a prosecutor in 78 B.C.E. and kept on climbing until he was elected Consul in 59 B.C.E. He conquered Gaul between 58 and 50 B.C.E. During his Gallic campaigns, Caesar dealt with Germanic tribes and discussed them in his Gallic War, which he wrote around 52-51 B.C.E to further his political career. A short section of the Gallic War is devoted to Germanic anthropology.

GALLIC WAR

New Moon

When Caesar asked the prisoners of war why Ariovistus did not fight, he found out about a German custom in which the women of German households would cast lots or perform auguries to decide whether they should go to battle. (5) These women also say that it is against divine law for the Germans to win a battle fought before the new moon.[1]

Death Lots

Vallerius said that the Germans cast lots three times right in front of him to decide whether or not to burn him alive right then or wait for some other time. Lucky lots let him go unscathed.[2]

Gods and Customs

German and Gallic customs differ. The Germans have no druids to preside over their religious affairs or perform sacrifices. (2) The Germans think that only visible things that bestow plain benefits are gods, such as the sun, the moon and Vulcan. They have not heard of the others. ... (4) Those who stay celibate the longest are praised the highest. They think celibacy increases their stature and builds power and muscle. (5) They are scandalized when a man has sex with a woman before he is twenty. But they do not keep sex a secret. Both males and females bathe in the same rivers clad in skimpy hides, cloaks or reindeer skins.[3]

---

[1] I, 50: (4)
[2] Ib 55, 7:
[3] Ib. VI, 21, 1:

3

STRABO

Strabo was a Greek geographer and historian who lived from around 64 B.C.E. to 23 C.E. His geographical writings cover the entire Roman Empire and some neighboring territories, including Germany.

GEOGRAPHY

Priests
The priest of the Chatti marched (in the triumphal procession of the neighboring Germans).[4]

Holy Kettle
The Cimbri sent their land's holiest cauldron to Augustus as a gift. They sought his friendship as well as amnesty for their previous transgression.[5]

Priestesses and Kettles
It is apparently customary for Cimbric women to go on military expeditions with their men. Priestesses with prophetic powers also go to war. The priestesses were old, dressed in white, and wore flaxen cloaks pinned with broaches. They went barefoot, and wore bronze belts. These priestesses came to the prisoners of war, fixed wreaths upon their heads, and took them to a ten-gallon cauldron. A priestess would ascend a ladder, ... and then reach over the kettle to slit the throats of each as they were raised to the kettle. Some of the priestesses rendered divinations from the rushing blood. Others inspected the victims' guts for signs of future tribal triumphs.[6]

VELLEIUS PATERCULUS

Valleius Paterculus, Roman veteran, politician, and historian lived from around 19 B.C.E until at least 30 C.E.; his history ends in 29 C.E. He began serving as a cavalry officer and a legate in Germany under Tiberius in 4 C.E.

An Old German Thinks Caesar is a God
We took a position on the closer side of the previously mentioned river. German weaponry flashed on the other side. They all fled when we executed naval maneuvers, except for one old and tall barbarian. You could tell he was noble by his clothes. He boarded one of those barbarian log carved canoes and paddled out into the middle of the river. There he shouted a request for permission to come over to our side. He wanted to come over to see Caesar, if he could do so without putting himself in danger. We gave him a chance. After disembarking on our shore he silently looked upon Caesar for some time. Suddenly he shouted, "Our young people are crazy! They idolize you as a god in your absence. But in your presence they would rather fear your military prowess than

---

[4] (rec. Kramer) VII, 4. 292:
[5] Ib. 2, 1 293L:
[6] Ib. 2 3. 294:

4

gain your patronage. Now, Caesar, by your beneficence, I have seen the divinity about which I had only heard about before. I have never known or hoped for a happier day in my life." He asked for, and received, permission to touch Caesar's hand. He got back into his canoe and kept looking back at Caesar as he paddled back to his own side.[7]

P. PAPINIUS STATIUS

Publius Papinius Statius lived between around 45 and 96 C.E. He was a major poet of the Latin silver age and served as Domition's court poet. The Silvae is a collection of 32 poems on a wide range of topics, and much of it is flattery of those who shaped his destiny.

SILVAE

The Priestess Veleda
It would be tedious to tell all about the northern armies on the rebellious Rhine, about how Veleda prayed when she was taken prisoner, or how you gloriously took the city after you vanquished the Dacians, or, about how Fortune herself was not surprised when you, Gallicus, were chosen for such an exalted rank.[8]

P. CORNELIUS TACITUS

Cornelius Tacitus lived between 56 and 115 C.E. He rose from the equestrian order to become a senator. He was an orator and a writer. He wrote several important historical works. Our excerpts are taken from three of them, including the Germania, The Histories, *and the* Annals.

The Germania *is a sort of anthropology concerning the customs, origins, and geography of the Germans. Unlike the anthropology and sociology of today, the* Germania *does not make a pretense of scientific detachment. Tacitus'* Germania *carries a moral message for the Roman people; the noble savages of Germany exhibit some of the same virtues as the Romans did during the Republican era. It also portrays the Germans as a people currently lacking certain Roman virtues, and warns that the Germans would truly be dangerous were they to gain these other virtues. Tacitus favored the conquest of Germany as a means of eliminating the German threat. Caesar's conquest and elimination of the Gallic threat in the first century B.C.E. were proof enough of the efficacy of this practice. Tacitus' Germans love freedom and have a strong sense of family values and honor.*

---

[7] (ed. Ellis II, 7):
[8] (ed. Klotz) I, 4, 89 s.:

GERMANIA

Tuisto, The Earth God
Old songs are the Germans' only way of recording history. They worship the earth-sprung god Tuisto with such songs. They say that Tuisto has a son called Mannus who was the progenitor of mankind. They also say he has three sons whose names are given to the other three German tribes; including the Ingvaeones who are nearest the ocean, the Hermiones, who are centrally located, and the Istaevones.[9]

Barditus, the Rebel Yell, and Hercules
Hercules is said to have walked among them. Before a battle they sing that Hercules is the strongest man. They also sing songs called "Barditii." These songs get them stoked up for the coming fray and augur the battle's outcome. From the sound they generate they can tell whether they are going to be scared or be brave. It seems like a chorus of virility more than a chorus of voices. They try to generate a tonal ferocity and an interrupted roar. They raise their shields to their mouths to generate an echo that increases the fullness and depth of the racket.[10]

Twin Horses
They like the old coins . . . especially those impressed with images of two-horse chariots. They also prefer silver to gold.[11]

Running Away
They take the bodies of their slain even from the battlefields on which the outcome is not yet certain. . . . A man who disgracefully throws down his shield in battle is barred from sacrifices and public meetings.[12]

Priests, Statues and Groves
The priests are the only ones who may grant permission for the infliction of other punishments. Such judgments are regarded as if they were divine mandates from the gods warding their campaigns, unlike a general's orders. They also bring to battle statues and symbols from their sacred groves.[13]

Women Are More Spiritual
They think women are somehow sacred and provident. They heed their women. They long thought that Veleda was a goddess. They also worshipped Albruin and many other women as actual goddesses rather than honoring them in mere admiration.[14]

---

[9] (ed. Halm-Andersen) 2:
[10] Ib. 3:
[11] ib. 5:
[12] Ib. 6:
[13] Ib. 7:
[14] Ib. 8:

Gods

They regard Mercury most highly of all the gods. Human sacrifices in his honor are lawful on certain days. Certain beasts are given to Mars and Hercules in sacrifice. Some Suebi also sacrifice to Isis. Her symbol is a liburnian ship. I do not know how or why this foreign divinity came to be worshipped there.[15]

Groves and Temples

They do not think it is fitting to enclose the Gods' heavenly might in walls or to depict them with any likeness of a human face. They hallow sacred groves and woods. They name these remote places after their gods and go to them in a state of religious awe.

Lot Casting

The Germans consult lots and auspices frequently. Their method is simple. They cut the branch of a fruit tree into tines differentiated by certain symbols. They scatter the tines randomly across a white cloth. Priests perform this function at public events and the household fathers preside in domestic contexts. Either way, the diviner first prays to the gods. He looks up to the heavens and raises three tines individually and interprets them by the symbols etched onto them. If the lots are negative, they do not consult them again during that day. If positive, then they make further divinations.[16]

Other Divination

They also divine by the chirping and flights of birds. They take warnings and predictions from horses. They have other methods as well. They feed certain white horses at public expense in sacred groves and woods. Performing tasks for mortals has never defiled these horses. They harness these horses to a sacred wain[17]. The king, or other village leader, interprets the horses' whinnies and snorts. No other folk relies so heavily on auguries. This is true for nobles and priests as well as for humble folk. Nobles think that they are the ministers of the gods and that their horses share knowledge with the gods.

They determine the outcome of serious wars with another type of augury. They somehow catch an enemy warrior and set him in single combat against one of their own. Both combatants use their own tribal armor and weapons. The outcome is taken as an omen.

They gather on certain days, barring unforeseen circumstances. They hold these conventions when the moon is full or new. They think these times are the best for initiating business transactions.[18]

---

[15] Ib. 9:

[16] Ib. 10:

[17] 'Wain' is an archaic word for a wagon or cart, as in 'hay wain.' I use this word as a variation, not because it more accurately reflects the sense of the Latin.

[18] ib. 11

Hang Traitors

They hang traitors and turncoats from trees. They submerge cowards, the unwarlike, and perverts in swamps. They heap wicker over them and pile on rocks to sink them into the mud. The difference in punishment follows a principle: display crimes and hide disgraces.[19]

Dowries, Marriages and Exchanging Gifts

The husband gives a dowry to the wife rather than the other way around. Parents and kinfolk ratify the gifts. The gifts given are not meant to ornament or please the bride. These gifts include things like oxen, a horse and bridal, a shield, a spear and sword. In return the gift, the husband acquires a wife, and she brings to the husband a gift of weapons. This gift exchange is central to the holy marital bond; sacred rituals hallow the union under the blessings of the presiding marriage gods. The bride is expected to remember that she also may have to endure the hazards of war or exercise manlike virtue. The marriage ceremonies that hallow the marriage at its beginning remind the wife that she enters her husband's home to share work and danger and that she will share the agonies and adventures of war and peace alike. These gifts, including the horse ready for riding, the ox-team and the weapons symbolize this. . . . The bride receives these gifts to hand down to her children to pass on to their wives who may then pass them on to their grand children.[20]

Uncledom

Some tribes regard the relationship between a man and his sister's children as being more sacred and close than his relation to his own children. That is why they sometimes try to take nephews as hostages instead of sons.[21]

Hospitality

It is thought sinful to turn any guest from one's door. The host gives his guest the best meal he can afford. After entertaining the guest, the host performs the additional service of accompanying the guest to the next home where the guest may be entertained. . . . Customarily, when the visitor leaves, he is allowed to ask for anything he wants. The host in turn, does not hesitate to ask for a gift in exchange. They love presents.[22]

Naked Sword Dances and Dice

They have the same kind of public spectacle, every single time, at all of their festal gatherings. Trained youths dance naked among swords and spears aimed at them. . . . They play dice seriously. . . . They will wager their own freedom on one final cast.[23]

Bring Out Your Dead

Their funerals are fairly simple. Their custom is to cremate noble bodies with special kinds of wood. They sometimes pile the deceased's armor, or even his horse, onto the

---

[19] ib. 12
[20] ib. 18
[21] ib. 20:
[22] ib. 21:
[23] ib. 24:

pyre, but they do not add incenses or garments. They raise a sod mound, but reject monuments made with great labor, thinking they are too heavy for the departed. Their tears and laments end quickly, but their sorrow and grief lingers. The women cry, the men remember.[24]

Teenage Fashion Statements and Initiation

Here is something normal for the Chatti, which the other tribes do only for a personal display of audacity. The Chatti teenagers let their hair and beards grow. After slaying their first enemy, they cut it all off and give it to manly virtue (*virtus*). They stand over the their slaughter and plunder to unveil their faces. They declare that they have paid the price of their birthright and that they are now worthy of their country and their parents. The cowards and unworthy remain in squalor. The bravest also wear an iron ring, which is to them a sign of dishonor, like chains. They remove their rings after their first kill. This is common among the Chatti. These insignia sing out the wearer's status to enemies and kin alike.[25]

Hercules

A common story is that Hercules is responsible for these pillars. Whether or not Hercules ever visited these shores or this is just a story like others that attribute everything to his might, Drusus Germanicus was audacious. Obstructions prevented him from further investigating the sea of Hercules. No one else attempted such investigations. It came to be considered holier and more reverent to believe in the acts of Gods than to know about them.[26]

Suebian Knot

The Suebi comb their hair to the side of their head and tie it in a knot. This knot is a mark of their tribe and it separates them from other Germans. This is how they tell the slaves from the free. Other Germanic tribes do not often do this, except that their kids sometimes do it because they have Suebian kin, or, more often, to imitate the Suebes. The Suebes wear their shaggy hair twisted back and sometimes knotted on the head even when it is graying. The leaders wear more elaborate hairstyles. This style is not meant to be beautiful or intended to get them laid. They do it to intimidate their enemies before a fight.[27]

The Semnon Fetter Grove

The Semnones are said to be the oldest and noblest of the Suebi. Their religion reinforces this belief. Kinfolk related by blood all gather in a wood at certain times. Their ancestors' offerings and ancient awe have hallowed this wood. Here they celebrate the awesome beginning of their rite with a human sacrifice. Every one who goes into this grove has to be tied with a rope. This subservience honors the might of the god. If someone falls he cannot just get up and leave. Nothing doing. He has to roll around on the ground instead. Their superstitious notion is that in this place dwells the all-ruling

---

[24] ib. 27:
[25] ib. 31
[26] ib. 34:
[27] ib. 38:

god and that everything else is subject and obedient to this god. They also think their tribe sprang from this place.[28]

Nerthus, Goddess of Peace and Love

Rivers and forests surround the Reudingi, the Aviones, the Angles, the Varini, the Eudoses, the Suardones and the Nuitones. There is nothing special about them individually, but they all share the veneration of the earth mother, Nerthus. They think she has a hand in human affairs and goes about among the folk. There is a sacred grove on an island in the ocean where there is a wagon draped with a sheet. This wagon is given to Nerthus. Only one priest has the authority to touch it. When he knows that the goddess is imminent in the temple, cows draw her wagon, and the priest follows her with profound respect. They hold big parties in those places she deems worthy of her presence. On these occasions, the people put their weapons in storage and go about unarmed. Love, peace, and quiet hold sway on these occasions. When the priest finds out that the goddess has had enough of human company, he returns the wain to her temple. Believe it or not, when they return, slaves wash the wain and the goddess in a secret lake. Then they drown those slaves in the same waters. There is a fear of the arcane in this custom. In awe they stupidly revere things that are only seen by folks who die for having done so, such as this spring.[29]

Divine Brothers

The Narhavales have a grove for an ancient rite. The officiating priests wear women's clothes. In Roman tradition the Gods so honored would be Castor and Pollux. This is also characteristic of the god Alcis. They worship these gods as youthful brothers. They do not make statues of them, but there is still evidence of imported religious practices.

The Harrii Get Scary

The Harrii are stronger and more ferocious than the aforementioned peoples. They cultivate their ferocity with skill and timing. They blacken their shields, dye their bodies, and strike on dark nights. Like an army of ghouls, they use scary shadows to strike terror into the their enemies' hearts. Enemies cannot stand up to the shock of their infernal appearances. In all battles, the eyes are conquered first.[30]

Mother Goddess and Boar Symbols

Therefore on the right-hand shore of the Suevian seashore live the Aestuii. They have Sueve-like customs and a language like that of the Britains. They worship the mother of the Gods. Her worshippers wear boar images as a sign of their devotion. Her worshippers get protection from this warding symbol instead of from arms.[31]

---

[28] ib. 39.
[29] ib. 40
[30] ib. 43:
[31] ib. 45:

THE HISTORIES

Feasting and Politicking in a Sacred Grove

Civilis called the tribe's leaders and its boldest commoners to what seemed to be a banquet in a sacred grove. When night fell and Civilis saw that that folks were warm with joy, he gave a speech.[32]

Loyalty Oaths

Civilis had them all swear loyalty oaths in a barbarian rite involving customary curses against oath breakers.[33]

Beast Shapes in Groves

Here were the veteran cohorts' battle standards, there were the shapes of the wild beasts they brought from their sacred groves.[34]

Red Dyed Hair

After this battle against the Romans, Civilis swore a barbarous oath to comb his hair forward, dye it red and not to cut it until he had shattered the legions.[35]

Veleda Rules

They sent the Roman legate, Municius Lupercus, to Veleda, along with other gifts. Veleda was a single woman who ruled widely over the Bructerian folk. It is an ancient custom among the Germans to regard many of their women as prophetic. When their superstition increases, they even regard them as goddesses, and so they regarded Veleda since she had predicted the Germans' good fortune and the destruction of the legions.[36]

Veleda's High Tower

They answered thus: . . . Veleda and Civilis shall judge which agreement they will ratify. . . . Thus the Tencteri sent a legate to Civilis and Veleda along with gifts and they got a judgment satisfactory to the Agrippinenses (People of Cologne). But they were not allowed to see or speak with Veleda in person. They cloistered Veleda to increase her religious mystique. She was ensconced in a high turret. One of her relatives was selected to carry her decisions and answers as if she were the Gods' intermediary.[37]

---

[32] (Rec. Halm-Andersen) IV. 14
[33] ib. 15
[34] ib. 22
[35] ib. 61
[36] ib. 61
[37] ib. 65

Land Wights

Civilis did not organize his battle formations silently. He called upon the battleground itself to witness their valor. . . . The Rhineland and the German Gods were in sight: and it was in their names that they began the battle.[38]

Veleda Given Roman Ships

The enemy towed away the captured ships in full daylight and brought the praetorian trireme (Roman Ship) up the river Lupia as a gift to Veleda.[39]

Cerialis sent messengers to the Batavians on the sly and offered forgiveness to Civilis. He advised Veleda and her kin to change the fortune of their wars as they had been total disasters so far. He asked her to do the Romans a favor.[40]

ANNALS

Tamfana
They destroyed sacred and profane places alike, including the temple of Tamfana, which the Marsi frequented the most.[41]

Roman Standards in Groves
I know that the Roman battle standards hang in Germany's holy groves given to their ancestral gods.[42]

Groves and Altars
Varus' first camp showed the work of three legions by its broad circuit and its commanders' quarters. A wrecked rampart and a shallow trench showed where the last remnant had stood its ground. . . . Splintered shafts and horses' limbs were strewn about. Human heads were fastened to tree trunks. Barbaric altars stood in the holy groves where the Germans slaughtered the tribunes and the first ranked centurions.[43]

Ariminius
Caesar crossed the Weser and found out from a deserter where Ariminius intended to do battle. They planned a night attack on the camp as soon as the other folks arrived.[44]

Idistavis
They were raging and demanded a fight. They were led to a field called Idistavis.[45]

---

[38] ib. V, 17
[39] ib. 22:
[40] Ib. 24:
[41] (ed. Halm-Andersen) I, 51)
[42] ib. 59:
[43] ib. 61:
[44] ib. II, 12:
[45] ib. 16:

Budahenna

Deserters told them that nine hundred Romans died in a grove called Budehenna because they tried to drag the engagement out to the next day.[46]

The Sun

Boiscalus looked up to the sun and called on all the heavens. As if he was speaking directly to them, he asked whether they liked seeing the land so desolated.[47]

Sacred Salt

War between the Hermunduri and the Chatti broke out that same summer. Both sides tried to take a brackish river which had been their mutual border. Besides an innate tendency to resolve all their differences with weapons, they thought that this river was very close to the heavens where the gods could better hear human prayers at that river. They thought the salt to be the gods' gift because of the manner in which it was obtained. In other rivers and woods salt is left by dried seawater. But there the salt could be obtained by pouring water on a wood fire. They though that the salt there came from the mixture of contrary elements, namely fire and water. The Hermunduri won the war and this loss was catastrophic for the Chatti. Each side had vowed to sacrifice the other to Mars and Mercury in the event of victory. To honor this vow, they gave men, horses, and armor to the gods in sacrifice.[48]

SEXTUS JULIUS FRONTINUS

Sextus Julius Frontinus lived from 35 to 103. Frontinus held various administrative offices in Rome and the Empire and wrote about aqueducts and military strategies.

STRATEGIES

Waning Moon

In Gaul, Caesar found out that Ariovistus, the German King, would not fight when the moon was waning. It was as if it was one of their laws. That is why Caesar committed his army at that time. He beat the Germans because they were burdened by their religion.[49]

C. SUETONIUS TRANQUILLUS

Suetonius was a Roman biographer and social historian who lived between around 69 and 122. His gossipy history of the first eleven emperors was shocking in its time. He wrote numerous unusual tracts on topics such as famous prostitutes, sports history, theater, oaths, mutants, authors, and famous men.

---

[46] ib. IV, 73:
[47] ib. XIII 55:
[48] ib. 57:
[49] Ib. 24:

LIVES OF THE CAESARS

The Phantom Barbarian Lady
Drusus campaigned in Reatia and Germany, first as a quaestor, and later as a praetor. He was the first Roman Commander to sail to the North Sea. Also, with great effort, he built canals beyond the Rhine that still bear his name. Drusus cut down enemies in frequent engagements and drove them deep into the wilderness of the interior. He did not stop until the larger than life phantom form of a barbarian lady told him in Latin to stop.[50]

A Seeress
He was suspected of killing his mother by keeping her from food while she was sick. A Chatti seeress had assured him that he would have a long and stable reign if he outlived his mother.[51]

A Diviner
He condemned a German diviner to be executed at dawn for interpreting a lightning strike as a sign of political change.[52]

PLUTARCH

The Greek biographer, Plutarch, lived between around 46 and 121. Plutarch wrote a series of parallel lives in which he compared the lives of great generals, statesmen and orators in Greek and Roman history. He held various posts in the government of the empire under the emperor Trajan, and held municipal offices in the Greek city of Chaeronea. Plutarch also studied and taught philosophy.

LIFE OF CAESAR

Seeresses
Their priestesses' prophecies discouraged the Germans. These priestesses take auguries from the whirling and splashing of river waters. These seeresses told them not fight until the new moon.[53]

MARIUS

The Cimbric Bronze Bull
The Cimbri attacked and took the fortress on the other side of the river Atiso. The Germans were so impressed by the Romans' exceptional bravery that they freed those who would swear oaths before a bronze bull. The Cimbri thought that the Romans' defense of the fort was worthy of their own fatherland. The Romans later captured that bull, and they hauled it off as the main plunder for their victory, or so the story has it.[54]

---

[50] (Ed. Ihm) V, *Claudius*, 1, 2:
[51] Ib. VII, *Vitellius*, 14, 5:
[52] Ib. VIII, *Domitian*, 16, 1:
[53] (ed. Sintenis) 19:
[54] (ed. Ziegler) 23:

APPIAN

Appian, the Alexandrian historian, lived in the second century and wrote a history of Rome from the republic to his own time.

ROMAN HISTORY

Afterlife
Caesar conquered the Germans, who, along with Ariovistus, disdained death in the hope of an afterlife and took the initiative.[55]

CLEMENT OF ALEXANDRIA

Clement lived from around 150 to 211. Clement was a Christian with Gnostic leanings. He wrote polemical tracts promoting Christianity and his theological opinions.

STROMATEIS

German Holy Women
The Germans have holy women who observe and divine signs from the eddies and splashing noises of river waters and thereby foretell fated things. They kept the Germans from fighting before the new moon.[56]

CASSIUS DIO

Cassius Dio lived from around 155 to 235 C.E. and wrote a history of Rome in Greek. The history begins with Aeneas' arrival in Italy and ends in his own time. He held several political posts in the Roman government and became a senator around 180.

ROMAN HISTORY

The Phantom Lady Again
Drusus met a lady who was larger than life. She asked him: "Where do you think you are going, Ravenous Drusus? Fate has decided that you will never see this land in its entirety. Get out of here! The end of your work is drawing near." I am unable to dispute this story, but it is certainly amazing that such talk should come from a divinity. Drusus soon left. A disease cut him down before he got to the Rhine, in spite of his hasty departure.[57]

---

[55] (ed. Mendelsohn), 4 <u>On the Celts</u>, 3:

[56] (Ed. Stahlin) I. 15, 72, 3:

[57] (ed. Melber) LV, I, 35:

Ganna, German Priestess

Masyas, the Semnone king, and Ganna, the German priestess who took over after Veleda, both visited Domition. After he had honored them, they left.[58]

AMMIANUS MARCELLINUS

The Roman Historian, Ammianus Marcellinus, lived from around 330 to 400. He wrote a history of Rome that picked up where Tacitus left off, at the reign of Nerva, and concluded the history with the reign of Valens. The history deals with some German campaigns. Ammianus was a pagan in an age when paganism was no longer cool, or safe.

BOOK OF DEEDS

Bad Omens
The Alamanni held counsel over recent developments. The rigor with which they had resisted was softening, and they sent leaders to ask for peace and forgiveness for their transgressions. They did this either because of bad omens or because sacrificial auspices prohibited combat.[59]

A Feather in His Cap
Chonodomarius started the whole disturbance. He wore flame colored feathers on the top of his helmet riding before the left flank.[60]

Sword Worship
King Vitrodor, Vituaris' son, and Agilimund, his head noble, along with other nobles, judges, and the leaders of various other tribes, drew their swords. They worshipped these swords as deities and swore their loyalty oaths by them.[61]

Blame the King for Bad Harvests
The Burgundian kings are usually called Hendinos, and by the authority of ancient tradition are impeached if their battle luck or the land's fertility fails. This is like the Egyptians who also blame their rulers for unfortunate events. The Burgundians call their head priest 'Sinistus.' The *sinistus* holds this post for life, safe from the hazards that endanger kings.[62]

---

[58] ib. (ed. Boissevain) LXVII, 5, 3:
[59] ed. XIV, 10, 9
[60] ib. XVI 12, 24
[61] ib. XVII, 12, 21
[62] ib. XXVIII, 5 14

CLAUDIAN

Claudian Claudianus, a poet and administrator, was born in Alexandria in 370 and died around 404. He gained influence and political posts by writing poems in praise of the western emperor Honorius and Honorius' German general Stilicho. He wrote a panegyric celebrating Stilicho's consulship as well as that of Honorius and a work on Stilicho's arrival in Rome. He also wrote poems condemning the eastern Emperor Arcadius, further endearing him to his patrons.

STILICHO'S CONSULSHIP

Groves
You won with so little time. So many battles and so little blood. You went as if the moon were waning but came back as if it were full. You made the Rhine gentle with its horns broken. You made it safe to hunt in the vast silence of the distant Hyrcanian forest and in those hoary holy groves, so awesome in their spiritual power. They once thought their trees were so holy, but our axes felled them with impunity. The barbarians once worshipped them as if they were divine.[63]

GOTHIC WAR

Alaric Hears a Voice
His burning pride broke forth in angry words . . . "The Gods drove me to these actions. I do not go in for birds and dreams. But I heard plainly a voice coming from the holy grove. 'Do not delay, Alaric! Cross the Italian Alps. Be brave and you will take the city.'"[64]

EUNAPIUS

Eunapius, Greek philosopher, historian, and rhetorician, lived from around 345 to 414.

Fragment 12:

The Camaboi all prayed to their Gods and their leaders invoked them verbally.[65]

VIGILIUS, BISHOP OF TAPSUS

Vigilius was the Bishop of Tapsus, which was a Roman province in North Africa. Little is known about Vigilius, except that he attended a church council in Carthage called in 485 by Hunneric, the Vandal king. The Vandals had invaded Gaul in 406 and then invaded North Africa in 429 and ruled that province by 435. Catholic and Arian bishops attended the council. Vigilius may have gone to Constantinople after the Arians exiled

---

[63] ed. Koch, M.G., Auct. Ant. X) 1, 281 s

[64] ed. Schroff) 520 s

[65] (Dindorf, Historici Greaci Minores I, 221 De Boor, Legislative Excerpts, I 593):

the Catholic bishops. *He wrote several anti-Arian works, including the Two Books Against the Arian Heretic Palladius which recounts the arguments over the Arian Christology made at the Council of Aquilaea in 381. This work takes the form of a dialogue and includes the arguments attributed to the Catholic Bishop Ambrose as well as the arguments of the Arian Bishop, Palladius.*

LETTER FROM THE COUNCIL OF AQUILEIA TO THE EMPERORS GRATIAN, VALENTINIAN AND THEODOSIUS

Gothic Fashions Blasphemous

What can we say about Attalus' teacher, Valens? When he was near the bishops' council he opted not to attend. He did not want to have to explain his bad deeds now that his country has been conquered. He profaned himself by the Gothic impiety of wearing armbands and a neck torque. He dared come before us, and in full view of the Roman army, in traditional Gothic dress. This gear is definitely sacrilegious; not just for a bishop, but for any Christian. The only Romans who do not shun these Gothic traditions are those priests who practice the Gothic blasphemy.[66]

AUGUSTINE

Augustine, the Bishop of Hippo, wrote City of God to refute the proposition that Rome had been sacked in 410 by the Visigoths because it had forsaken its own gods in favor a novel foreign religion.

CITY OF GOD

If they had won, how loudly, and with what mockery they would have bragged. Radegasius would have boasted that he was so powerful, and that he had conquered, because he had worshipped and sacrificed to the gods every day; and that the Romans could not because they were Christians. When he was nearing Rome, he was bragging and saying that he was invincible to those who did not sacrifice to the Roman gods and were not even allowed to do so. These stories spread all over the land. But Rome is where God's majesty would smite him.[67]

OROSIUS

The Spanish priest, Paulus Orosius, wrote History Against the Pagans around 418 to argue that all the calamities that destroyed the Roman Empire, especially the Gothic sack of Rome, were not caused by the abandonment of the Roman Gods in favor of Christianity. Augustine suggested this project to him, as you might have guessed.

---

[66] Two Books Against Palladius the Arian, II, 8 (Migne, P.L. LXII, 465) The gothic blasphemy referred to here is Arian Christianity.
[67] ed. Dombart-Kalb V, 23

HISTORIES

Buried Plunder

The enemies (Cimbri and Teutons) . . . had a strange and damnable religious practice. They gathered up all the plunder they took in war and gave it to the earth.[68]

Offerings Made after Winning

The Germans threw their clothes onto the ground. They tossed their gold and silver into the river. They hacked apart soldiers' cuirasses and destroyed horse trappings. They drowned their horses in the rushing waters. They fastened nooses about men's necks and strung them up in trees. That way the winner had no plunder and the defeated were given no quarter. . . . The women asked the magistrate to spare their lives if they remained celibate and served as vestal virgins. He denied their request. They smashed their children on the rocks and killed themselves with swords and nooses. The Tigurones and the Ambrones did these things. The Teutonic and Cimbric women committed suicide with iron meant for enemies.

Radegasius was far and away the biggest of all barbarians, ancient or modern. Radegasius and over 200,000 Goths hit Italy with a sudden attack. The heathen, Scutha, led this indomitable army and gave Roman blood to his gods. He followed the traditional customs of these barbarian peoples in so doing.[69]

SOZOMEN

Sozomen lived from around 400 to 450. He was an attorney in Constantinople and began writing a church history in 439. This history begins in 324 and ends in 425. Most sources indicate that the Arian Germans were highly tolerant of religious diversity.

ECCLESIASTICAL HISTORY

An Arian Inquisition

They say Athaneric's men loaded a cart with an idol and drew it to the tents of suspected Christians. Suspects were tortured and ordered to worship the idol and to offer sacrifice. They burned the stubborn in their dwellings.[70]

APOLLINARIS SIDONIUS

The Gallic Bishop and writer Sidonius Apollinaris lived between 430 and 479. His writings give us a glimpse into the life of Gallic aristocrats in the waning years of the empire. Germans, including Franks, Burgundians and Visigoths were living in various parts of Gaul in Sidonius' time. The Visigoths were dominant in Gaul after 455. From

---

[68] ed. Zangenmeister I, 16 5 x
[69] ib. VII, 37, 4 s
[70] Ed. Hussey VI, 37, 13

19

the writings of Sidonius it appears that life went on as usual for many aristocrats, in spite of the Germanic occupation.

EPISTLES

Lots and Prisoners of War
When the Saxons want to unfurl their sails, hoist their biting anchors from enemy waters, and cast off from the continent to sail home, they customarily crucify or drown in sacrifice every tenth prisoner of war. It is really too bad that a superstitious ceremony has them dealing out the injustice of death by drawing lots. These blood offerings defile them rather than purify them. Those instigating these terrible killings think they are undertaking a religious duty and that it is better to torture a person than to get ransom money for him.[71]

LEX SALICA

This law code of the Salian Franks was probably issued by Clovis in the beginning of the 6th Century, possibly between 506 and 511. At the beginning of Clovis' reign in 481, the Franks lived in northeastern Gaul or France where they had been established by the Romans as a buffer between themselves and other Germanic tribes. By the end of Clovis' reign, the Franks held much of Gaul. There are various versions of the code, and the earliest version shows no Christian influence. The Lex Salica is mainly a penal code and contains sixty-five titles.

Votive Hogs
If someone steals a votive hog, and it is proven that the hog was in fact votive, the thief pays 700 dinarii or 17 solidi for the pig.[72]

Crossroads
If someone goes to the crossroads to meet a man whose enemies have cut off his head and hands, he shall pay out 4,000 dinarii at the law hill.[73]

Pulling a Head Out
If someone pulls a head out of a marsh, and some enemies of the head's owner had cast the head into the marsh, and if he does so without permission from a judge or the man who cast it in, he pays 15 solidi.[74]

Marrying Widows:
If a man wants to marry the wife a dying man, when, as is customary, the dying man divorces his wife, then he must bring a shield to the thing before the judge or local official, as set forth by the Thunginus (judge), or the centenarius (local official).[75]

---

[71] (rec. Mohr) VIII, 6, 15
[72] II, 12 (ed. Behrend, 2. ed. 5)
[73] XLI, 8 (1, 1. 81)
[74] Add. 2
[75] Ib. XLIV (1. 1. 95 s.)

ADOPTING INTO AN INHERITANCE

The following practice is to be observed and agreed to. Let the *thunginus* (judge) or *centenarius* (local official) preside at the thing. The adoptor shall let three men ask him questions. After that he shall bring forth the adoptee and cast a staff into his lap. He shall then state how much property he wishes to give, and the manner in which he wants it given. Then he must stay in his house and receive as guests the three men who questioned him and they need to see to it that the adoptor has as much property as he says he will give. Afterwards the adoptee shall do the same thing before witnesses. The adoptor must state before either the king or the lawful assembly what his property is to be. He must take the staff to the assembly within twelve months and there give it to the one who has been proclaimed his heir. The adoptor shall there cast it into the lap of the adoptee and with it the amount entrusted to him, neither more nor less.

If any one objects, three witnesses must declare under oath that they were present at the thing and that the *centenarius* or the *thunginus* presided. They must then declare how much property the man intended to give and that he cast the staff into the lap of the man he intended to be his heir. They must then say how much property the man intended to give and that he cast the staff into the lap of the adoptee. They must then name the man who cast the staff and the man who received the staff and thereby became the adoptor's heir. Three more witnesses must state how much property the adoptor intended to give, and that he cast the staff into the lap of the adoptee. Then they must name the man who cast the staff, and the man who received the staff and thereby became the adoptor's heir. Another three witnesses must declare under oath that they stayed in the adoptor/donor's house and that three or more guests gathered and ate gruel at his table, that they had gathered as witnesses, and that they had thanked him. Three more witnesses must say these things to the king, or else in public before a *thunginus* or *centenarius*. They must state that this man cast the staff into the adoptee's lap and that the adoptee thereby became his heir. They must also establish that altogether there were nine witnesses.[76]

WITCHES

Brew Kettles

If someone accuses another of witchcraft (*strioporcium*) and he brings to the thing a cauldron in which he says the accused makes brews, then let the accused pay in fine 2,500 dinarii or 63 solidii.[77]

Stria

If someone accuses a freeborn woman of witchcraft (*stria*), and does not prove it at the thing, let him pay in fine thrice 700 dinarii or 189 solidii.[78]

---

[76] Ib. XLVI (1. 1. 95 s.)
[77] ib. LXIV. (1. 1. 129 s.): 1
[78] 2.

21

Wasting

If someone causes another person to waste away by using witchcraft, and he can prove it at the thing, the accused pays in fine 1,008 dinarii or 200 solidii.[79]

CAPITULARY

Perjury

If someone thinks another has perjured himself and he can prove it, the perjurer pays 15 solidii. If he cannot prove it, the accuser pays 15 solidi. If he wants to press the case further, the issue will be tried in a fight.[80]

EXTRAVAGENTIA

False Charters

If someone takes a charter to the thing and another man says that it is false, but the possessor insists that it is valid and not false, then here's what happens; the accuser pierces the document with an awl and brings forth seven witnesses who will state that it is false. He needs one witness for each defense witness claiming that it is valid. If sixty-nine sworn witnesses state that it is false, the document shall be declared false. But if the charter's possessor will not comply with this ruling, the two sides will each choose a duelist from among the witnesses and try the case in a duel.[81]

BURGUNDIAN LAWS

The Burgundians inhabited Southeastern Gaul. Gundoband, his son Sigismund, and Godomer issued these Burgundians laws from 483 to 532. Gundabad issued a separate code for Romans living under Burgundian rule.

BOOK OF CONSTITUTIONS

Judicial Duel

It appears that some people are corrupt. Having no case, or being naturally greedy, they often swear oaths in matters about which they are uncertain, as well as swearing false oaths regarding affairs about which they are certain. We propose the following law to discourage such crimes. When a defendant appears before the people and denies under oath that he owes what the plaintiff demands, or pleads not guilty to the charges brought against him, the litigation should be terminated as follows: when the party to whom the oath was offered refuses to accept the oath then that party shall declare that the adversary's credibility can be refuted in duel. If the accused will not agree, then the suit will be tried in fight. The champions for the duel shall be drawn from among the witnesses. Let God decide this suit. If someone thinks they are totally sure of the truth, then he should fight without hesitation. But if the witness offering the oath is defeated,

---

[79] Add.
[80] VI, 15 (1. 1. 159)
[81] B IV (1. 1. 167)

22

then all the witnesses who swore shall pay 300-solidii right then. If the one refusing to accept the oath is slain, then whatever he owed is to be paid back nine-fold from his estate to the winner. Let's be glad in truth and not in lies.[82]

ENNODIUS

Magnus Felix Ennodius lived from around 473 to 521, spending most of his life in Ticinum and Milan. He was a scholar, a prolific writer of prose and poetry, and a rhetorician.

In 507 the pope commissioned Ennodius to write a work thanking and praising the Ostrogothic King, Theoderic, for his tolerance of Catholics and Catholicism. Theoderic belonged to the Arian sect of Christianity, as did most of the German Christians at that time. The original Arian theology maintained that Christ was a man who became a son of God through his own works. The Arian Germans were generally tolerant of other faiths. Sozomen aside, it was generally when they converted to Catholicism that the German Christians began inflicting cruel barbarities upon non-conformists of all types. Ennodius became Ticinum's bishop in 513. Nevertheless, he was from an important Roman family and felt a strong bond to the pagan Roman traditions which he attempted to reconcile with Christianity.

THE LIFE OF BLESSED ANTHONY

The Lottery
The Franks, Herulians, and the Saxons were waging their wars with all kinds of atrocities. These tribes have a superstitious religious practice. They think that they need to slaughter their own kind to get their gods' divine favor. They thought for sure that shedding innocent blood would make the Gods happy. So they sacrificed their own kinfolk. They burn any one designated by inscriptions in a religious rite as if it was really a great sacrifice. They think that their god's anger will cease if they slaughter the pious and that the crime scene becomes a place of grace.[83]

COUNCIL OF BISHOP ASPASIUS OF ELLUSANUS (Held in 551)

Folks who Enchant Drinking Horns
On folks who enchant drinking horns by the inspiration of the devil and are said to be wizards. Men of rank are to be excommunicated and thus driven from the church's threshold. Slaves shall be bludgeoned to death by a judge. If they pretend to have been corrected and to fear God, cane them.[84]

---

[82] CMV (Composed in 502 C.E.) (M.G., Leg. Sect. I, 75 s.)

[83] 13 s. (M. G., Auct. Ant. VII, 187)

[84] c. 3 (M.G., Leg. Sect. III, I, 114)

JORDANES

Jordanes was a Romanized Goth who lived near the Danube in the mid 6th century. His Gothic history is partially based upon the lost twelve-volume work of Cassiodorus.

THE DEEDS AND ORIGINS OF THE GOTHS

Heruli
But the Danes, who have the same racial origins, drove the Heruli from their homes. The Heruli are the tallest of the nations of Scandza.[85]

Womb of Nations
In ancient times, King Berig is said to have led the Goths out of that island of Scandza as from a hive of races or womb of nations.[86]

No Sacking Roman Temples
When at last they got into the city of Rome, Alaric specifically instructed his army to loot Rome, but not burn it like a bunch of barbarians. Nor did he allow them to defile the sacred places. [87]

Alaric's Funeral
The folk affectionately mourned Alaric's death. They diverted the river Busentius' course somewhere around Consentia. Busentia's wholesome waters flow from the mountain near Consentia. Some war captives were led into the river's bed to dig a grave for Alaric. They buried Alaric in this hole, along with great riches, and then diverted the river back to its usual course. They killed the war captives to keep anyone from finding Alaric's grave. The Visigothic kingdom passed to his relative, Athaulf. Athaulf was handsome and had a great soul. He was not tall but his face and physique were attractive.[88]

Tyranny
Gelmer dethroned and killed Gaiseric. He ruined his race by ignoring his ancestor's wisdom and establishing a tyranny.[89]

The heathen hand (Vandals) had cut the nation (Africa) from the Empire long before.[90]

Nobility Hard to Hide
Beremund arrived showing the strong mind for which he was well known, but was wisely silent about his noble ancestry. He knew that kings never trust folks with royal ancestry. He went incognito to keep from frightening the nobility. King Theodorid

---

[85] III (23)
[86] IV (25)
[87] XXX (156)
[88] XXX (158)
[89] XXXIII (170)
[90] XXXIII (172)

granted extraordinary distinctions to Beremund and his son by giving them seats at his table and counsel. The king bestowed these honors on Beremund for his courageous heart and forceful mind. Unlike his noble ancestry, Beremund could not conceal these qualities. [91]

Pilleati

The Goths were therefore wiser than other barbarian peoples and were very much like the Greeks, according to Dio, who wrote their history and annals of the Goths in Greek. Dio tells us that the noble line from which kings and priests were derived were known as Tarabostesi and then as Pilleati. The Getes were so highly regarded that it was said that Mars himself, who is called the God of war in the myths of poets, had been born among them. Thus, according to Virgil, "Father Gradavius rules the Getic Fields." [92]

Mars and War Prisoners

The Goths have always worshipped Mars with severe rituals. They thought that they should please a war god with human blood. They gave to him the first fruits of war. They stripped enemies of their arms and hung them in trees in sacrifice to him. They were more deeply religious than other nations because the worship of this god seemed ancestral. [93]

Ancestor Songs

In ancient times they sang about their ancestors' exploits. Their songs were accompanied by the cithara. [94] They sang about Eterpamara, Hanala, Fritigern, Vidigoia, and others who are very famous among them. [95]

The King is not Forgotten

When the Gothic king, Tanausius, died, the Goths worshipped him as one of their gods. [96]

Harp Playing Priests Beat Macedonians

Then the Gothic priests known as Holy Men unexpectedly threw open Odessa's city gates and went forth against them. They carried harps and wore white robes. They sang songs of prayer to their ancestral gods petitioning the gods be favorable and beat back the Macedonians. The Macedonians were flabbergasted when they saw the Gothic priests marching forward with such confidence. You might say that the unarmed terrorized the armed. [97]

Dicinius, Gothic Philosopher

Their only safety, their security, and their advantage, derived from this: they did whatever their wise man, Dicincus, counseled. They deemed it advisable to strive for

---

[91] XXXIII (175)
[92] (40)
[93] (41)
[94] A type of stringed instrument.
[95] (42)
[96] VI (48)
[97] VIII (65)

this. Dicinius was an able master of philosophy. When he found that their minds were loyal to him in everything, and that they had an innate capacity, he taught them the whole of philosophy. He also taught them ethics and thereby curbed their barbarous traditions. He taught them physics and had them live naturally under their own laws. They possess these laws, known as the 'Belagines,' even today. He taught them logic and gave them an ability in reasoning that surpassed all other nations. He also taught them practical wisdom and convinced them to perform good deeds. He taught them theoretical wisdom and pressed them to ponder the twelve signs and planetary courses passing through them, as well as the whole body of astronomy. He showed them how the lunar disc wanes and waxes and how the sun's burning globe is bigger than our planet earth. He expounded on the names of the three hundred and forty six stars and the signs to which they belong and their courses through heaven's arching vault, as they speed from their risings to their settings.[98]

I ask you to reflect on what a delight it was for these courageous men to receive instruction in philosophy when war offered them so little spare time. You may have seen one Goth surveying the positions of heavenly bodies and you might have seen another Goth studying plants and bushes. Here stood one studying the moon's waning and waxing, while yet another studied the sun's workings and saw how the heavenly bodies speeding eastward are spun around and brought back to the west by the revolving heavens.[99]

Dicinius taught the Goths these and other things. By his wisdom he gained such a great reputation among them that he ruled both commoners and kings. He selected those of noblest ancestry and the wisest and taught them theology. He asked them to worship particular deities and sacred sites. He gave the name "pilleati" to the priests he ordained, probably because they performed sacrifices wearing those tiaras on their heads, known to us as "pillei."[100]

But he had them call the others of their nation "Capillati." The Goths accepted this name and valued it greatly. They still use it today in their songs.[101]

After Dicinius died, they esteemed Comosicus nearly as much for he was no less knowledgeable. They considered him their priest and king because of his wisdom. He was also a just judge.[102]

Ansis
Because of their great victory in this land, which they attributed to the good luck of their leaders, they called their leaders Ansis, which meant that they were not just men but demigods.[103]

---

[98] XI (9)
[99] XI (70)
[100] XI (71)
[101] XI (72)
[102] XI (72)
[103] XIII (78)

Ansila
Achiulf then begat Ansila and Ediulf.[104]

First Spear Thrown in the Battle
"I will cast the battle's first spear at our foe. If any is able to stand idle while Attila is battling, he will die." Burning with this speech, they rushed into the fray.[105]

Heruli
Odoacer, the Torciling king, soon invaded Italy at the head of the Sciri, the Heruli, and other allied nations.[106]

Back-Birth
Mathelusia's second husband Germanus was a cousin of the Emperor Justinian. Germanus brought her to Constantinople and she bore him a posthumous son and named him Germanus.[107]

Heruli
The Heruli functioned as light troops.[108]

Lots
The Goths all went to Thiudimer, their King, and clamored and pleaded with him to go to war in any direction he desired. King Thiudimer called for his brother. They cast lots and the king ordered him to invade Italy, which was then ruled by Emperor Glycerius. Thiudimer said that since he was greater he would go east to face a greater nation.[109]

PROCOPIUS

The Byzantine historian Procopius lived from the late 5th or early 6th century to sometime after 526. He served in the Emperor Justinian's army under the General Belisarius in wars against the Persians, the Vandals in Africa, and the Goths in Italy. He wrote about these wars in his De Bellis. You can read about the Vandals in Books 3-4 and about the Goths in Books 5-7.

GOTHIC WARS

Funerary Suicide
The Herulians have lived in a region beyond the Ister (Danube) . . . since ancient times. They worshiped lots of Gods. They thought that law sanctioned human sacrifice. When a Herulian died, his wife would hang herself with a noose by her husband's grave so that

---

[104] XIV (79)
[105] XXXIX (206)
[106] XLVI (242)
[107] XLVI (252)
[108] XLIX (261)
[109] LVI (283)

folks would remember her as a good woman. If she did not do this she would live out her remaining years as a disgrace and as a source of embarrassment to her husband's family.[110]

Forty Days of Night in Thule

Every year in Thule a wondrous thing happens. The sun hovers above the earth for forty-two days without setting. This occurs every summer during the solstice. But in less than six months, during the winter solstice, it is consumed by the night's boundaries and does not appear at all for another forty days. Depression strikes the whole people for the whole time as the darkness keeps them from having dealings with one another.

I wanted to see this island's reported wonders for myself, but did not get a chance. I did ask folks coming back from the island how they could tell the length of the days during the times when the sun neither rises nor sets. They gave a fair and accurate answer. They said that even though the sun did not set for forty days, it did appear to people in the east and west. When the sun gets to the point where it once rose, they reckon one day has passed. During the long night they tell time by the moon and stars. When they figure that thirty-five days of the long night have passed, they designate people to send to the mountain peaks to wait for the first glimpse of the sun. When they see the first glimpse, they announce to the people below that the sun will rise in five days. The whole of the folk has a huge party in the dark when it get the news. This is the Thulians's biggest party of the year. The islanders seem to be terrified that the sun might not come back at all, even though it comes back every single year. [111]

Christian Franks Sacrifice and Practice Divination

The Franks took the bridge and sacrificed all the Gothic women they found there. They cast the bodies of the fallen into the river. These barbarians converted to Christianity but keep much of their traditional life. Not only do they have human sacrifices, but they do other illegal things, such as practice divination.[112]

Sacrifice to their Ancestors

Such is life for the barbarians. But the other Thulian folk are not much different from other peoples. They worship lots of gods and spirits that dwell in waters, springs, and rivers. They sacrifice to their ancestors. They think the best sacrifice for Ares to be the first prisoner taken in a battle. Ares is their greatest god. Besides the usual means of sacrifice, they hang their victims from trees, toss them into thorns, or find some other exceedingly horrible death.[113]

A Little Bird Told Him

Hermegisclus, a Varnian ruled them. . . . When he was with the most renowned Varnian, a bird chirped loudly from a tree and thereby gave him a prophecy. We do not know whether it was really the bird that told him or whether he actually got his

---

[110] II 14, 1 s. (ed. Haury, 208 s.)
[111] ib. 15, 5 s. (1. 1. 215 s. 218)
[112] ib. 25, 9 s. (1. 1. 262)
[113] 23.

information elsewhere. He told those around him that he knew he was going to die forty days later because a bird told him.[114]

Soul Barge

They say that spirits of the dead are taken to Brittia. I will tell you how, since I have heard so many such stories told in earnest. I personally think these stories come from dreams. Many villages lie on the coast across from Brittia. Fisherman, farmers and the merchants who trade with Brittia live there. Though subjects of the Franks, they do not have to pay tribute because they have performed a task for the Franks since ancient times. I will tell you about it. The inhabitants say they lead away the souls of the dead, and that they all take turns. Each night one team relieves another. They go home at night and sleep until they are called for duty. Late in the night they hear a knocking at their door, and an indistinct voice calling them to their duty. They get up instantly and go to the shore. They do this job even though they are not entirely sure what is compelling them. They find unmanned skiffs at the shore. These skiffs are not theirs, and are not like theirs. They board the boats and man the oars. They find the skiffs so weighed down with passengers that the boats are wet up to gunwales and oarlocks, which are no more than a fingers breadth above the water. The passengers are invisible, but the Brittians row for an hour and disembark on Brittia. When they sail with their own boats using oars instead of sails, they have trouble making the voyage in a day and a night. After their passengers have disembarked, they quickly embark on the skiffs. The boats are now so light that the water does not reach above the keels and they ride on top of the waves. But they do not see anybody sitting with them or leaving. They say that they hear a voice calling the names of the departed souls to those who will receive them. This voice also tells of their reputations and names their fathers. If some passengers are women, the voice names their husbands. This is the way the events are described by the natives, in any case.[115]

PRECEPT OF KING CHILDIBERT

King Childebert issued this legislation between 533 and558.

Idols in Fields

It is our decree that only one warning will be given and then each must immediately remove from their fields any satanic and artificial figures and idols. Nor may they stop bishops from wrecking those idols. ... Concerns have been expressed about folks who pursue unfortunate and blasphemous practices. These things hurt God and these sins are killing those folks. They drink and sing bawdy songs all night long on Easter, Christmas and on other feasts. They even dance through towns on Sundays.[116]

---

[114] ib. IV, 20 5 s. (1. 1. 590 X 598 s.)
[115] 48
[116] Boretius, *Capitulari regni Francorum,* MGH, Leges II, 1(Hannover 1883) pp. 2-3.

COUNCIL OF AUXERRE

The Council of Auxerre was convened between 561 and 605. The pagan practices described herein seem to be a mixture of Germanic and pre-Germanic customs. I have selected passages that probably concern Germanic practices.

1. Wearing stag costumes on the kalends of January is not allowed. Nor are they to make satanic gifts. Favors are to be given then as on any other day.

3. Folks are not allowed to hold saints' vigils or make offerings to saints in their own homes, or to render oaths at sacred trees, springs, or in the woods. Anyone who wants to swear an oath, let him hold his vigil in the church and give to the poor or to church workers (*matriculae*). Nor shall they presume to make wooden feet or wooden sculptures of humans.

4. Folks are not allowed to consult diviners, auguries or people who claim to know the future. They are not allowed consult the "saints' lots" or those they make of bread or wood.

8. Do not let folks give at the altar in a Holy Sacrifice that concoction of honey and wine, *mellita,* which they call *mulsa.*

9. Choruses of either laymen or girls are not to sing in church or to celebrate feasts in church.

17. Do not let folks make religious offerings to people who have committed suicide by hanging themselves or hurling themselves from trees, by drowning themselves, stabbing themselves with iron, or killing themselves by any other means.[117]

AGATHIAS

The Byzantine lawyer, historian, and poet, Agathias, lived from around 536 to 582. His historical work covers the period from around 552-558 and was left unfinished.

HISTORIES

Groves and Sacrifices

Although the Alamans have their own traditions, they have a Frankish style government and civic administration. But their religion is different. The Alamans revere certain trees, rivers, hills and ravines. They behead horses, cattle and lots of other creatures as sacrifices as if such acts were divinely sanctioned. . . . I do not think that words can remedy the insanity and barbarity of such sacrificial rites, whether in the sacred groves of

---

[117] C. De Clercq, pp. 265-270.

the barbarians or the temples of the Greeks. I do not think any one really likes bloody altars and the savage slaughter of animals.[118]

They Did Not Listen to Their Seeress

These events threw the Franks into an even greater tumult. Their hearts were seething with rage and hastily readied for war. They could not restrain themselves. They were immeasurably brave and confident. They resolved not to tolerate further delay and to fight that same day. This, even though the Alamanic seeresses had warned them that if they fought that day they would get obliterated.[119]

GREGORY OF TOURS

Gregory became bishop of Tours in 573. He wrote several hagiographies, including Lives of the Fathers, and one history, The History of the Franks. The history's purpose was "to tell about wars between kings and their enemies, between the church and heathens, and between the church and heretics." As well as recording earlier Frankish history, Gregory tells of events in his own time; he was involved in many of the events he recounts.

LIVES OF THE FATHERS

Wooden Hands and Feet

In Cologne there is a temple where the barbarians give their first fruits and where they eat and drink until they puke. There they worship idols as if they were Gods. There they adore images as God and sculpted in wood limbs that were stricken with pain.[120]

HISTORY OF THE FRANKS

A Duel Instead of a War

The Vandals, led by King Gunderic, poured out of their own country and into Gaul. The Sueves, who were known as Alamans, followed them and took Galicia. A dispute arose between the two tribes over their shared borders. Both tribes armed and marched to battle. Right before they engaged, the Alamanic king made a speech. "How long are we going to let war ruin both our nations? I beg of you not to let both armies die. Instead, let a champion from each side fight for his own nation. The winners' folk takes the land without contest." All the folk on each side agreed to this so that a multitude would not have to die by the sword. King Gunderic died and King Transimund then succeeded him. The two champions fought, and the warrior representing the Vandals lost. When the champion died, Transimund promised to fulfill his oath and depart and promised that they would leave Spain as soon as they were ready.[121]

---

[118] I, 7 (Historici Graeci Minores II, 150 s.)

[119] ib. II, 6 (1. 1. 89)

[120] VI, 2 (M.G. Scr. Rer. Mer. I, 681)

[121] II, 2 (1. 1. 60)

Statues of Animals

The Franks seem to have always been given to crazy religious rites and have always dismissed God. They made figures depicting creatures of the forests and waters. They made images of birds, beasts and other things. Instead of worshipping God, they venerated and sacrificed to these idols.[122]

King Clovis Argues with his Wife about Theology and Baptism

Chlotild bore Clovis' first son. She wanted to baptize him and she would continuously badger Clovis, saying: "Your gods are nothing; they are unable to help themselves or others. They are carved out of stone, wood or some kind of metal. The names, which you gave them, were those of men, not of Gods. Take Saturn, who ran from his own son to avoid expulsion from his kingdom. Or how about Jupiter? He was an obscene perpetrator of all kinds of debauches. He debauched other men and even his own sister, who said: . . . 'at once the sister and wife of Jupiter' according to legend. And what can Mars and Mercury do? Their powers are just magical and unworthy of being called divine."

The king's mind was not moved any further toward belief by this speech. He replied: "All things were created by the command of our Gods and it is yours who have been shown capable of nothing. Moreover, let me point out that yours is not even of the race of Gods."

Meanwhile, the pious queen had her son baptized and given the name Ingmer. But just as he was baptized he died in his white robes. The king brimmed with rage over this and railed at the queen: "If the boy had been blessed in the name of the Gods he would have lived . . ."[123]

A Prophecy

Then Guntram told a servant to visit a certain lady he had known since Charibert's time. She had prophetic powers. He wanted to know his future. She foretold not only the day and the year, but also the exact hour, that Charibert would die. She sent a message to Guntram through his servants saying: "King Chilperic will die this year and King Merovech will take the entire kingdom and exclude his brothers from power. You will be the commander of the kingdom's armed forces for five years. In the sixth year, you will be made a bishop by the will of the townsfolk on the Loire's left bank. You will leave this world an old man."[124]

Herbs and a Paranoid Queen

Meanwhile, the queen found out that the boy died; he had been overwhelmed by sorcery and enchantments. She also learned that the prefect Mumulus had been involved in her son Theoderic's death. She had long hated Mumulus. Actually, he was in his house having dinner, when somebody from the court came to him and lamented that a boy he held dear had died of dysentery. The prefect replied: "I have here an herb, which can

---

[122] ib. 10 (1. 1. 77)
[123] ib. 29 (1. 1. 90 s.)
[124] ib. V, (1. 1. 203 s.)

cure a person of dysentery, no matter how ill or who he may be; provided the sick person brews a drink with this herb and quaffs it." These words kindled an even hotter rage in the queen's heart. She ordered several women of the parish seized. She had them flogged and tortured to force them to reveal the truth. They just made things up. They admitted to practicing witchcraft and to killing many people. Then they added something I cannot believe at all. "We sacrificed your son for the life of Mumulus." The queen racked them with even more terrible tortures. She beheaded some, others she burned, and some she broke on the rack, shattering their bones.

Then the queen left to stay with the king in Compeigne. There she told the king all she had heard about the prefect. The king sent servants to seize him. They chained, interrogated, and tortured him. They hung him from the rafters with his hands tied behind his back to interrogate him for witchcraft. He insisted that all he knew was that certain women supplied him with brews that were supposed to bring him into the good graces of the king and queen.[125]

A Broken Axle
Then Riguntha tearfully kissed her parents good-bye. An axle broke as the wagon went through the gate. Onlookers said: "This is a bad time. Forsooth!" They thought this a bad omen.[126]

More Omens
Claudius watched for omens as he rode; it was a Frankish custom. He found the omens inauspicious.[127]

Hallowed Staves
Then Gundovald sent two messengers to King Guntram. As accorded with Frankish religious tradition, he carried hallowed staves to protect himself from those seeking to harm him and to help him return from his mission with a favorable response.[128]

A Prophetic Vision
Then a woman announced to the Parisian townsfolk: "Get out of the city. Much of it is going to burn in a bad fire!" Many laughed at her; they said she had reached this conclusion by casting lots, or from an empty dream, or that she had been seized by a noontide demon. She replied: "That is not so. I saw it in a vision. I saw an ancient man leaving the basilica of St. Vincent. He held a wax candle in his hand and set fire to the merchants' houses as he came to them."[129]

---

[125] ib. VI (1. 1. 274 s.)
[126] ib. VI, 45 (1. 1. 285)
[127] ib. VII, 29 (1. 1. 308)
[128] ib. VII, 32 (1. 1. 312)
[129] ib.VIII, 333 (1. 1. 384 s.)

POPE GREGORY I, THE GREAT

Gregory was elected pope in 590 and remained pope until 604. He established missionary activity in England in 596 and sent St. Augustine to England under whose auspices a bishopric was eventually established in Canturbury. Gregory also encouraged missions among the Lombards. Meletius was a French Abbot on his way to Britain at the time Gregory wrote the famous Epistle XI in 601.

DIALOGUES

A Sacred Goat
Witnesses tell us that about fifteen years ago the Lombards captured forty rustics and tried to force them to eat sacrificial meat. But when they resisted and refused to touch the meat, the Lombards threatened to kill them. About the same time, the Lombards forced 400 other prisoners to partake in a pagan rite. In this ceremony, they sacrifice a goat head to the devil. They worshipped him by running in a circle singing a terrible song, and then adoring the idol by bowing their heads.[130]

LETTER TO BRUNICHILD (written in 597)

Trees and Idols
We encourage you to be sure to restrain your subjects from sacrificing to idols and worshipping trees. It has come to our attention that such practices are carried out in contradiction to divine will and that many Christians and church congregations oppose it. Therefore, they must desist from such practices. [131]

See to it that tree worshippers do not emerge and that they do not present sacrilegious sacrifices with animal heads.[132]

LETTER TO MELETIUS (written in 601)

Pope Says Turn Temples into Churches
When omnipotent God leads you to that most reverent of men, our brother, Bishop Augustine, tell him of the plans I have long had in mind for the Angles. The temples should not be destroyed, but the idols, which are housed in them, should be. Ready holy water to sprinkle in those temples. Then you can place altars and relics in those temples. If the temples are soundly constructed, then they need to be transformed from places of devil worship into places pleasing to God. When the folk finds its temples are still intact, it may abandon its error. Now they will know the true God and may also worship in their usual places. In these festivals they traditionally kill and sacrifice lots of cattle to demons. They should change the form of this solemnity such that their feast days become dedication days and martyrs' birthdays for the relics housed in the temples. Let the people make tents for themselves from the boughs of the trees around those churches

---

[130] III, 27 s. (M. G., Scr. Rer. Lang. 534)
[131] (M.G. Epist. II, 7)
[132] ib.

34

that used to be temples and celebrate their festivals as religious feasts. Do not let them sacrifice animals to demons. Make sure that they kill animals to eat themselves giving praise and thanks to God the provider of plenty. They will have some outward pleasures for themselves so that their minds will more readily know inward bliss. You cannot remove all the error from their minds at one time. Those striving for the summits must ascend in steps, not in leaps.[133]

BAUDONIVIA

Baudonivia was a nun in the Monastery of the Holy Cross at Poitier in the sixth century. She wrote a portion of theLife of Saint Radegund shortly after 600. She added her own stories of St. Radegund to a biography written by Venatius Fortunatus in the sixth century. Radegund was the daughter of a Thuringian king who was abducted by Clotaire I when he conquered Thuringia in 531. Radegund's uncle had slain her father and had also killed her brother. Clotaire forced Radegund to become his wife. She sought sanctuary at the monastery of Poitier where she became a nun. She died in 587.

LIFE OF SAINT RADEGUND

A Frankish Temple

The lady Altfrid invited Radegund to breakfast. Radegund started her trip with a retinue of 100. A little ways down the road, there stood a Frankish temple. It was not far from the road, and about a mile from the prosperous queen. When Radegund found out about it, she had her retinue burn it down. She thought it unjust that folks should revere such diabolical contrivances and disregard God in heaven. A multitude of Franks tried to stop the destruction of their temple. Armed with swords and clubs they came at her making a hellish racket. But the holy queen persevered in her plans and remained fixed on her horse. With Christ in her heart she refused to move until the temple was destroyed. Afterwards she made a speech saying that the people had now strengthened the peace among themselves.[134]

COUNCIL OF CLIPIACENSE

This council was convened in 626 or 627 in Paris in the Basilica of Mary the Mother of God located near a place called Clipiacense.

Idolatries

We know that there are Christians who take auguries; this is like the pagan crime. There are many who eat with pagans. It is best to persuade such people to abandon these old errors by admonishing them gently. But if they do not listen and they engage in sacrifices and idolatries, let them do penance.[135]

---

[133] (1. 1. 331)
[134] II, 2 (M. G. Scr. Rer. Mer. II, 380)
[135] c. 16 (M.G., Leg. Sect. III, 199)

COUNCIL OF REIMS

This council was convened by bishop Sonnato sometime between 627 and 630. Over forty Gallic bishops gathered at this council held in Reims.

Various Heathen Practices

Those found performing pagan religious practices, or auguries, or eating religious meals with the pagans, should be gently warned to abandon these pagan errors. If they do not heed you, let them do penance. [136]

CHRONICLE ATTRIBUTED TO FREDEGAR

Written between 642 and 658, this history of the Merovingian Franks was written to cover the period from circa 584, where Gregory of Tours leaves off, to circa 642. This chronicle began to be attributed to Fredegar in the 16ᵗʰ century.

The Lombard Story

In the time before the Lombards were called Lombards, they and their wives and children left Scandinavia and crossed the Danube. Scandinavia lies between the Ocean and the Danube.

When the Huns found out that a tribe was crossing the Danube and waging war against them, they wondered what tribe had presumed to cross into their territory. The Lombard women came up with a plan. They cut the hair from their heads and attached it to their jaws so that they would look like their men. Thus it would seem to the Huns that the Lombard host was quite large. A voice called out from one of the towers and is said to have shouted: "Those are some long beards!" The Lombards thought these words came from their own God, whom they fanatically called Woden. The Lombards shouted: "He who gave us our name granted victory!"[137]

JONAS OF BOBBIO (SUSA)

Jonas, a monk and hagiographer, was born at the end of the 6ᵗʰ century and died after 659. He wrote The Life of Columbanus around 642. He joined the monastery of Bobbio in 618 and worked under the abbots Attala and Bertulf. He did missionary work in Belgium and northern France. Some of Jonas' writings were source material for Bede. Columbanus was the abbot of Luxeuil and Bobbio. He was born in Ireland in 543 and died around 615. He was active in the Courts of Clotaire in Nuestria and Thuedobert of Austrasia. He pursued missionary work among the Seuves and Alamans.

---

[136] c. 14 (M.G., Leg. sect. III, I, 204 s.)
[137] III, 65 (M.G., Scr. Rer. Mer. II, 110)

LIFE OF COLUMBANUS

Springs
In Luxovium they built springs for special religious observances. They crowded the nearby forest with stone images that they had worshipped in terrible and impious rites in days of yore. They gave sacrifices to the idols in awful ceremonies.[138]

A Ceremony For Woden
The Sueves live there. When we went there and lingered among the inhabitants, we found out that they wanted to perform an evil sacrifice. They called for a big vat that held about twenty pecks when filled to the neck. They set the vat at the center of their gathering. God's man went over to them and asked what they were going to do with that vat. The said they were going to sacrifice to their God, Woden, whom others call Mercury.[139]

Burning down a Temple
At that time there was another monk, and he was named Meroveus. The Blessed Attalus ordered him to the city of Dertona. He went to a certain villa near the river Hiram, in accordance with his mission. At the Villa there was a temple among the trees. He heaped up a pile of wood around it like it was a funeral pyre.[140]

THE LIFE OF VIDAST (died around 540)

Ceremony with a Vat
He was amazed at what he saw at the lunch to which he had been invited. He entered the house and saw a vat filled to the neck, prepared for a traditional rite. He asked them why this vat stood in the middle of their house. They replied that some things are for Christians and others for heathens. They added that they were about to have a sacrifice as a part of a traditional rite. He denounced the practice and made the sign of the cross over the vat on account of its use in this rite. He called on Almighty God by name and blessed the vat with the help of faith and heaven's gift. Upon performing this benediction, his words destroyed the sacrificial vat. He picked up the wooden neck and dashed it against the pavement.[141]

ROTHAR'S EDICT

The Lombard Laws were written down after the Lombards had invaded Italy in 586. These laws applied to Northern and Central Italy which were under Lombard control. King Rothar issued the first codification of the Lombard Laws in 643. Rothar's Edict codifies 388 laws.

---

[138] I, 10 (rec. Krusch, Scr. rec. Germ. 1905, 169)
[139] 9b. 27 (1. 1. 213)
[140] ib. II, 25 (1. 1. 289)
[141] 7 (1. 1. 315)

Capital Crimes

When someone accuses another of a capital crime before the king, the accused may clear himself by swearing an oath. If both accused and accuser are present, the accused may clear himself of the charges by a *"camfio"* or judicial duel.[142]

Accusation of Witchcraft or Prostitution

On charges brought against a girl under a guardianship: If a man accuses a girl or a free woman under a guardianship of practicing witchcraft or prostitution, . . . if he perseveres in his accusation and insists that he can prove it, then let the case be tried by a *camfio* so that God can decide the issue.[143]

Murder Plots

If a woman plots to kill her husband either by herself or through the agency of another, she is to be given over to the husband who may dispose of her and her property as he sees fit. If she denies the charge, then her parents have the option of clearing her name by oath or *camfio*.[144]

Adultery

On the crime of adultery: If a man accuses another man of seducing his wife, the accused has the option of clearing himself by oath or *camfio*.[145]

Ownership

On possession: If somebody accuses another of illegally possessing his moveable or immoveable property, and the accused has had possession for more than five years, he may clear himself by oath or *camfio*.[146]

Swearing on Weapons

Oath Breaking: An oath is known to be broken when a person accused of such will not dare to swear on a consecrated bible or hallowed weapons, even when oath-helpers join him. If any oath-helpers withdraw from an oath, the oath is considered broken.[147]

Debt Collection

If someone tries to collect a debt against a recently deceased father, and the son claims that his father never owed such a debt, he shall offer an oath and its gravity shall correspond with the amount of money involved. He may swear an oath that his father did not owe such a debt, or defend himself in a duel, if he can.[148]

---

[142] 9 (M.G., Leg. Tom. IV, 13 s.)
[143] ib. 198 (1. 1. 48)
[144] ib. 202 (1. 1. 50)
[145] ib. 213 (1. 1. 52)
[146] ib. 228 (1. 1. 56 s.)
[147] ib. 363 (1. 1. 82)
[148] ib. 365 (1. 1. 84)

Unfair Herbs and Magic in Dueling
On Dueling: No man who fights in a *camfio* may have on his person herbs used in witchcraft or any similar such thing. Duelers may only bring the arms agreed on earlier.[149]

Witches
Let none presume to kill another's maid for being a witch (*striga* or *mascam*). Christians do not believe that it is possible to eat a living man from the inside.[150]

Accusation of Cowardice
If a man calls another man a coward in anger, and he cannot deny having done so . . . and if he persists, let him prove it in a *camfio*, if he can.[151]

THE ORIGIN OF THE LOMBARDS

This short history was written after the middle 7ᵗʰ century by an unknown author.

The Lombard Story
There is an island named Scandan and its name means 'destruction.' Many tribes dwell on this northern island. A small tribe named the Winiles dwelled among them. A Winile woman named Gambara had two sons named Ibor and Agio and these three ruled the Winiles. Ambri and Assi, the Vandal leaders came and told them to start paying tribute or fight. The three Winiles leaders replied that is better to fight than pay taxes to the Vandals.

Assi and Ambri, the Vandal leaders, then asked their God, Godan, whether they would win. Godan said: I will give victory to whomever I see first before the sun rises. Gambara and her two sons asked Frea, Godan's wife, to favor Winiles. Frea gave them a plan. They would go out with their women when the sun rose. The women would loosen their hair and wrap it around their faces so they would appear to have beards. Then the shining sun rose and Frea turned her sleeping husband's bed so that it was facing East. Then she awoke him. Godan looked out and saw the Winniles with their hairy faces and asked "who are those long beards?" Frea replied to Godan: "Just as you have given them a name, so you shall give them victory." He gave them victory, when he appeared. From then on, the Winniles have been called the Lombards.[152]

VISIGOTHIC LAW CODE

The Visigoths moved into Gaul as a Roman Federate Tribe around 418 and moved into Spain later in the 5ᵗʰ century. The Franks drove them out of Gaul in 507. King Euric issued the first written Visigothic laws between 466 and 485. King Recceswinth promulgated a set of laws in 654 which was revised in 681 C.E. The Visigoths originally

---

[149] ib. 368 (1. 1. 85)
[150] ib. 376 (1. 1. 87)
[151] ib. 381 (1. 1. 88)
[152] 1 (M. G., Scr. rer. Lang. 2 s.)

codified one set of Laws for themselves and a separate set for the conquered Spanish Romans. The Visigothic laws issued in 654 combined laws for Visigoths with laws for Romans. This twelve-section code includes 344 laws incorporated into the earlier laws of Recceswinth, Leovgild, and Chindaswinth.

Chastising Storm Bringers etc.

The following sorts are to be publicly flogged. They shall receive two hundred lashes, be disgracefully scalped and driven against their will through the neighboring villages so that others may learn by their example. These sorts are to be so dealt with any time they are found, by either a judge or a regional overseer: witches (*malefici*), storm bringers, those using incantations to bring hail into crops and vines, those who invoke demons and use incantations to confound men's minds, people who worship demons in night sacrifices.[153]

Stealing Coffins

If someone steals a dead man's coffin for a cure, the presiding judge shall pay 12 solidii to the dead man's next of kin.[154]

LOMBARD LAWS ADDED BY GRIMWALD

Nine laws were added to the Lombardic Law Code known as Edict of Rothar in 688. Here are three of them.

Slaves Cannot Challenge Owners To Duels

On Acquiring Title After Thirty Years. A male or female slave who is recognized as having served his or her lord for thirty years and because of pride, or by means of fraudulent claim, wants to belong to another man, may not challenge his master to a duel to claim his or her own person. No way.[155]

Freemen

If a freeman remains free for thirty years, let none harass him with challenges to duels. He gets to keep his freedom.[156]

Crimes by Wives

Crimes by Wives: If a person accuses his wife unjustly and without lawful cause of adultery or plotting to kill her husband, the accused may clear herself by her parents' oaths or by combat.[157]

---

[153] VI, 2, 4 (MG, SR Lang. 2 s.)
[154] XI, 2, 2 (1. 1. 259)
[155] 1. s. (M.G., Leg. Tom. IV 92)
[156] 2.
[157] 7. (1. 1. 94)

PENITENTIAL OF THEODORE

Books of Penitance seem to have originated in Wales and Ireland. They were common in Ireland in the 6th century. The Irish missions to the continent brought the use of penitentials to Germany. Theodore of Tarsus, The archbishop of Canturbury from 668-690, did not write this penitential, but responded to questions by the presbyter Eoda, who wrote down these responses. These were later edited by an unknown Englishman.

CANONS OF GREGORY

Demons
If someone shall sacrifice to demons in a minor way, he shall do one year of penance; if someone sacrifices to demons in a big way, he shall do penance for ten years.

Roofs and Ovens
A women who places her daughter on the roof or in the oven to cure a fever shall do penance for five years.

Burning Grain
Those who burn grain where a man has died for their health and household shall do penance for five years.

Singing Spells
If a woman sings evil chants or divinations . . . A person who conducts auguries, seeks omens from birds or dreams, or performs any divinations according to heathen tradition, or invites these sorts into their homes, or seeks the delusions of sorcerers.

Sacrificial Food
If a person eats sacrificial food and confesses, let the priest take the following factors into consideration.[158]

ALAMANNIC LAWS

Composed in the first part of the 8th century, this code replaced an earlier Alammanic code known as the Pactis Legis Alammanorum that had been issued around 613.

Accusations
When a freeman accuses another of a capital crime before a king or a duke and cannot prove the charge and he is the only one to make the accusation, the defendant may defend himself by the sword against the accuser.[159]

---

[158] 115 (Schmitz, Bussbucher II, 535)
[159] XLIII (M. G., Leg. Sect. 1 I, 103)

41

Refusing to Give a Dowry

If the dead husband's next of kin refuses to give a dowry to that woman, which is illegal, he must swear an oath with five oath helpers, or both sides shall draw swords in a duel to decide the issue. If she is able to get the property by combat, let it never be recovered from her. After her death let her husband and children keep it ever after.[160]

Denying Manslaughter

If somebody kills and denies killing, he needs eleven oath helpers to swear for him on consecrated weapons.[161]

BAVARIAN LAWS

Around 500, the Bavarians formed out of a confederation of the Marcomanni and Quadi. The Bavarians lost their freedom to the Franks in the 6th century and endured periods of Frankish influence. The Bavarian Laws were promulgated between 744 and 748 under Duke Tassilo III who ruled until 788. This was a time of increasing Frankish influence.

Plotting to Kill a Duke

If somebody plots to kill a duke appointed to the region by the king or by the people themselves, and the charge is proved to the point that it cannot be refuted, his life is to be given to the duke and his property to the state. This should not be done casually. The charge must be proven true. It should not be proven with only one witness, but rather it should be done with three witnesses of the same rank. But if one witness denies the charge, and the other affirms it, then let them have a fight so that God can give victory to the side that is right.[162]

Stealing Oxen

If someone is accused of stealing a domesticated ox, or a milk cow, then he can have six oath helpers swear with him or two fighters can have a duel.[163]

Arson

If a man wants to deny burning a house, he can swear an oath with twelve oath helpers, or have a duel.[164]

Warning Signs

If someone takes a sign that was meant as a warning or to block a forbidden road, or for protecting or enclosing a grazing ground, and this is a sign known as a *"wiffam"* that has

---

[160] LVI, 2 (1. 1. 113)
[161] LXXXI (1. 1. 149)
[162] II, 1 (M.G., Leg. Tom. III, 281)
[163] IX, 2 (1. 1. 303)
[164] X, 4 (1. 1. 309)

been set up in accordance with ancient traditions, he shall pay one solidi in recompense.[165]

Boundary Markers
Common markers are a common source of discord. . . . and if no proof is found for either side . . . The parties may take turns swearing what we call the "*wehadic*." The champions are not to draw lots. Instead, God will give strength and victory to the owner of the designated portion of land.[166]

Building Permits
There is not going to be any testimony about this type of building, but the builder may defend it by law. If the builder wants to protect a building and there is no fence, let him throw an axe valued at one saiga, and throw it at midday to both the east and the west. He may build a fence to the north only as far as the shadow, unless a dispute needs to be resolved.[167]

Crop Magic
If anyone wields magic against another's crops, and this is discovered, . . . and if he denies the charge, let him swear an oath with twelve oath helpers or let him gird a champion to fight for him.[168]

False Oaths
If a man swears falsely, let him pay recompense to him whose case suffered as a result. Let him pay twelve solidi in compensation and let him set the record straight.[169]

Damaging Corpses
If eagles and other birds find a corpse, as they often do, and start lacerating it, a man shooting at the birds and hitting the dead body instead has to pay twelve solidi, if anyone finds out.[170]

Damaging Corpses
Also, anyone who damages a dead body killed by another shall pay twelve solidi. Cutting off heads, hands, feet, ears, or other body parts, which a perpetrator knows to be grounds for a blood feud has to pay whether the injury is great or small.[171]

On Magicians
On auguries, enchanters, diviners, storm bringers, or people working other kinds of magic; the holy council agrees that wherever they are caught, they should be bound and

---

[165] 18 (1. 1. 309)
[166] XII, 8 (1. 1. 312 s.)
[167] 10 (1. 1. 313 s.)
[168] XIII, 8 (1. 1. 315 s.)
[169] XVIII, 6 (1. 1. 327)
[170] XIX, 5 s. (1. 1. 328 s.)
[171] 6.

brought before the archbishop of the diocese. He will be subjected to a thorough investigation to get him to admit to his bad deeds.[172]

LAWS OF LUITPRAND

The Lombard king, Luitprand, issued his own laws between 717 and 735 and added them to the Edict of Rothair and the Additions of Grimwald.

Deceitful Suits

There are those depraved folks who bring others to duels deceitfully. Such an accused shall swear an oath stating that he does not issue his challenge deceitfully, but is quite certain in his suspicion of a theft, fire or some other crime which demands a challenge to a duel. If he will not swear this oath, the case shall not be judged, and it shall be determined by combat.[173]

Seers

If someone ignores god's wrath and goes to a seer (*ariolus*) or seeress (*ariola*) either to get auspices or for receiving any kind of response, let him pay to the royal treasury half what he would be worth if he were killed. He shall also do penance as described in the canon.[174]

Trees

If a person worships trees and springs that the rustics think sacred, or casts sacrilegious spells, he must likewise pay half his value to the royal fisc.[175]

Sorcerers

If anyone knows sorcerers or sorceresses, and does not inform on them, or hides them, or does not inform on their clients, they are subject to the above punishment as well.[176]

Auguries

If someone sends male or female slaves to get auguries or otherwise consult with sorcerers or sorceresses, he is subject to this punishment.[177]

Sorcerers

If a male or female slave consults sorcerers or sorceresses without the permission or authorization of their lord, then their lord should sell them in another province. If the lord does not sell them, he is subject to the penalty described above.

---

[172] (1. 1. 471)
[173] 71 (M. G. Leg. Tom. IV, 136)
[174] 84 (1. 1. 141 s)
[175] 84 (1. 1. 141 s)
[176] 84 (1. 1. 141 s)
[177] 84 (1. 1. 141 s)

On Poisoning

Our judges decreed that whoever kills a freeman with poison forfeits his goods. Some men misuse this law by fraudulently claiming that a relative who died in bed was poisoned. This seems serious to us because a man can lose all his property in a single duel. Therefore, the accuser must prove in a duel that one of his relatives was killed by poison in this kind of case. After the duel, he must swear an oath on a bible and swear that his claim is not fraudulent and that he is certain that his suspicion is correct. After this, he may prosecute the case according to the ancient tradition.

If the defendant or his champion loses the duel, he shall not forfeit all his property. Instead he shall pay the accuser the value of the man who fell in combat in accordance with earlier laws on compensations. Although we are uncertain about the judgment of God in these cases and we have heard that many men lose their cases unjustly through combat, the Lombard customs prevent us from changing this law.[178]

Property Disputes

Sometimes folks living in the same village argue about fields, vineyards, meadow land, forest, or other property, and one party gathers his men to expel the other and declares: "We hereby expel you and enclose our territory." We rule that if this causes the injury or death to the one they are driving out, they shall pay compensation for the man's wounds or death in accordance with an earlier edict issued by Rothar, our Glorious king.[179]

Trespassing

If someone goes onto another's property without a public official's authorization, saying that it ought to be his, and he is not able to prove that it should be his, then let him pay six solidi, just as if he planted a pole in foreign ground.[180]

PENITENTIAL OF EGBERT

Written between 721 and 731, this is another English penitential produced as a result of the Irish mission to England. Egbert was the archbishop of York and the brother of the Northumbrian king Edbert. Egbert died in 766.

Divination by Writings

If anybody erroneously observes lots and auguries as if they were sacred, or promises to tell the future through the inspection of some kind of writings; or, if someone offers an oath at a tree, and this is made known to the church, then let them be excommunicated from the church in which they are clerics or laity. If the guilty party is a cleric, he shall do penance for three years. If it is a layperson, two years or one and a half. Do not use this power when the case is doubtful because they think they can defend themselves with their clamors and witchcraft.[181]

---

[178] 118 (1. 1. 156)
[179] 134 (1. 1. 156)
[180] 148 (1. 1. 173)
[181] VIII, 1 (Schmitz, Bussbucher, I 581)

DANIEL, BISHOP OF WINCHESTER

Daniel held the West Saxon bishopric of Winchester from 705 to 744 and died in 745. He was a friend of Bede, Aldhelm and Boniface. Daniel supplied Bede with historical source material. Boniface often turned to Daniel for advice in his missionary work and two of Daniel's letters to Boniface have been preserved.

LETTER TO BONIFACE (Written between 723 and 724)

How to Debate Theology

Do not start out arguing over the genealogies of their gods. Go along with their assertions that their gods were born to other gods via sexual unions of male and female. Then you can demonstrate that these cannot be gods because they were born like men and did not exist before that. . . . Once you have made them admit their gods had a beginning, ask them whether the world had a beginning or whether it has always existed. Why do they sacrifice to those gods if they are so powerful? . . . If their gods need such things, how come they do not just get better gods. If their gods do not need such sacrifices, then it is unnecessary to even think of trying to please them by giving sacrifices. . . .

Know Their Myths

You should occasionally mention their myths and compare their superstitions with our christian teachings, in a subtle way. That way the pagans may realize how silly their notions really are as they see that we know about their revolting rites and myths.

You should remind the pagans that Christianity rules the world and that they are a small minority who still follow the old fashioned ideas.[182]

POPE GREGORY II

Gregory II was pope from 731 to 741. He backed missionary activity in Germany and especially the missionaries Boniface and Corbinian, whom he made bishops in Germany in 722.

LETTER TO THE ENTIRE THURINGIAN NATION: (Circa 724)

Idol Worship

You shall not worship idols or sacrifice meat because this is not acceptable to God.[183]

LETTER TO BONIFACE (Circa 726)

---

[182] (Tangle, Die Briefe des Heilegen Bonifatius u. Lullus 40)

[183] (Tangl, Die Breife des Heiligen Bonifatius u. Lullus)

Sacrificial Meals

On sacrificial meals: . . . You asked whether the faithful are allowed to eat such food if they make the sign of the cross over it.[184]

THE VENERABLE BEDE

Bede was the first great English historian and spent virtually his entire life in the vicinity of the monasteries of Wearmouth and Jarrow. He was educated at Wearmouth. Although he became a bishop at 33, he remained devoted to study, writing and teaching. He completed the Ecclesiastical History in 731 when he was about sixty years old. His Ecclesiastical History tells the story of the Anglo-Saxon church.

ECCLESIASTICAL HISTORY

Hengist and Horsa

It is said that the first Angle kings were the two brothers Hengist and Horsa. The Britains killed Horsa later in a war. To this day a monument stands in eastern Kent with Horsa's name on it. They were the sons of Wictgils, son of Vecta, son of Woden, from whose sire descend the royal families of many kingdoms.[185]

Heathen Priest Bashes Temples

Coifi was the king's highest priest. He stated: . . . "Your highness, let us condemn, anathematize and burn those useless temples." . . . When the king asked who would dare to be the first to profane those fence guarded temples with their idols and their altars, Coifi replied: "I will." Coifi cast off his useless superstition and asked the king for a stallion warhorse and weapons with which to ride forth to smash the idols. Priests who presided at pagan ceremonies were not allowed to bear arms and could only ride mares. . . . Coifi wasted no time. As he reached the temple, he threw the spear at the temple to profane it. We were glad in this acknowledgement of the true god. He ordered the men who accompanied him to destroy and burn the temple and its fences. You can still see this place where the idols used to stand. It is just a little ways east of York and beyond the river Derwent and is called Goodmanham. It was here that the priest desecrated and destroyed the altars, which he himself had once consecrated. He destroyed them by the inspiration of the true god.[186]

King Redwald Sets Christian Altar Next to Pagan Altar

Redwald, Earpwald's father, Redwald, had been baptized long ago in Kent, but it did no good. When he got back home, his wife and some of his pernicious counselors urged him to abandon the true faith. He fell even lower than before. Like the ancient Samaritans, he sought to worship both the old gods and Christ. In the same shrine he kept an alter for the holy sacrifice of Christ right next to a small alter on which he made sacrificial offerings to demons. King Aldwulf, who ruled that region during our own time, said that this shrine was still standing in his day and that he had seen it when he was

---

[184] (726 C.E.) (1. 1. 46)
[185] Ecclesiastical History I, 15 (rec. Plummer I, 31)
[186] ib. II, 13 (1. 1. 111 s.)

47

just a boy. King Redwald had proud ancestry but performed ignoble deeds. He was the son of Tytila, son of Wuffa, and the East Anglian kings are known as Wuffings after his name.[187]

Loosing Letters
By saying these masses, he always got loose right away whenever anyone chained him. The nobleman keeping him prisoner was amazed. He asked why he could not be fettered and whether he had any loosing letters (*literas solutorius*).[188]

ON THE SEASONS

Easter, The Goddess

The Romans called the first month of the year January, but the English called it *Giuli.* . . . The English year started on December the 25th which is when we celebrate Christ's nativity. This night which is so holy to us, the heathens used to call '*Modranecht*' or 'Mother Night. We suspect they so named this night on account of the rituals the performed then. . . . *Solmonath* can be called 'cake month' because of the cakes they gave to their Gods in that month. '*Hrethamonath*' was so named because they gave offering to the Goddess Hrethe in that month. Easter, the name of the month known now as Pascal, used to be the name of the Angles' goddess. They used to honor this holiday with her name. Now we call Pascal by her name, and use the traditional name of an ancient custom to refer to a new holiday. . . . *Halegmonath* means the 'month of holy festivals.' '*Blodmonath*' or the 'sacrificial month' is so-called because in that month they killed cattle and offered them to their Gods.

POPE GREGORY III

Pope from 731 to 741, Gregory backed missionary activity in Germany, especially that of Boniface, who eventually became the metropolitan bishop of Germany. He made an alliance with the Franks in the face of a Lombard threat and thereby established a strong bond between the Franks and the Papacy.

LETTER TO BONIFACE

Heathen Baptisms
Those baptized in the heathen way shall be rebaptized in the name of the trinity.

Horse Meat
You say that some folks eat the meat of both wild and domesticated horses. This tradition is reprehensible and unclean. You must stamp out this practice wherever you find it with Christ's help and impose appropriate penances on miscreants.

---

[187] ib II 15
[188] ib IV. 22

Baptisms by Jupiter's Priests

We decree that those who are not sure whether they have been baptized, or were baptized by a priest who sacrifices to Jupiter or eats sacrificial meat. . . . You also reported that some people sell their slaves away from the faith to pagans who sacrifice them.[189]

LETTER TO ALL THE NOBLES AND FOLK

Divinations, prophetic lots, sacrificial offerings to the dead whether at springs or groves; auguries, charms, incantations, and magic, are all sacrilegious witchcraft. These things are going on all the time in your country. Turn to God with all your heart and throw all that away.[190]

THE GERMAN COUNCIL

This is Part of a letter from St. Boniface, Bishop of Mainz, to Lul, one of his disciples, who succeeded him. This letter concerns decisions made at a council in Germany.

Need Fires

We decree that God's bishops shall be sure that God's folk not do pagan things; the canons insist on this. The count is the church's defender and shall help the bishop out with this. God's folk must trash all pagan garbage, including divination by lots, augury, incantation, prophecies, sacrificial offerings to the dead, amulets, and human sacrifices. Idiots render hostile sacrifices in pagan rites right next to churches in the name of holy martyrs or God's confessors. Bishops are to diligently stop all these pagan rites, including those sacrificial fires they call "need fires."[191]

INDEX OF PAGAN SUPERSTITIONS

This 8th century list of superstitions comes from the Codex Vatican Pal. Lat. 577, and is entitled the Indiculus Superstitionem et Paganorum. Its date and authorship are not certain. Some think it is a product of Boniface since it follows canons issued at a church council held in 742 under Carloman and Boniface.[192]

1. Sacrilege at the tombs of dead people.
2. Sacrilegious songs known as 'dadsias' that are made for dead people
3. Pollutions in February.
4. Small houses that are really temples.
5. Sacrileges involving churches.
6. Sacred forests known as "Nimidas."
7. Things done over rocks.

---

[189] (732 C.E.) (Tangl, Die Briefe des Heiligen Bonifatius u. Lullus 51)
[190] (738 C.E.) (1. 1. 69)
[191] C. 5 (Tangl, Die Briefe des Heiligen Bonifatius u. Lullus 100)
[192] (M.G. Leg. Sect. II, I, 223) *See F. Sehetbauer Das Kirchenrecht bei Bonifatius. Also see Hefele-Leclercq, III, ii, 836-43.*

8. Rites to Mercury and Jupiter.
9. Sacrifices made to saints.
10. Knots and amulets.
11. Sacrificial Springs.
12. Incantations.
13. Auguries taken from the sneezing or the dung of birds, horses or oxen.
14. Sorcerers and diviners
15. "Need fires" which are fires made by rubbing sticks together.
16. Animal heads.
17. Pagan observances involving the hearth or the initiation of business matters.
18. Obscure places they hold sacred and where they worship.
19. Bedding hay that good men call 'Holy Mary's'.
20. Holidays celebrated in honor of Jupiter and Mercury.
21. A lunar eclipse, when they shout "Victory to you, Moon!"
22. Tempests, horns, and spoons.
23. Trenches around villas.
24. The pagan practices called "yrias" in which they cut garments and shoes.
25. Folks who carve images of just any dead person and claim they are actually saints.
26. Figures made of dough.
27. Making statues out of clothing.
28. Carrying statues through fields.
29. Wooden feet and hands that are seen in pagan rites.
30. The Pagan notion that women control the moon so that they can steal men's hearts.

POPE ZACHARY

Pope from 741 to 752, Zachary negotiated with Lombards and Franks. He brought about peace with the Lombards. He also promoted Boniface's missionary efforts in Germany and made him the papal legate there in 741. The following is excerpted from one of Zacharius' letters to Boniface written circa 748.

LETTER TO BONIFACE

Goats and Bulls
You wrote about the sacrilegious priests who sacrifice bulls and goats to pagan Gods and about sacrifices to the dead.[193]

LIFE OF ELIGIUS

Eligius was a royal goldsmith, treasurer and mint master under Clotaire II and Dagaobert. He died in 660. This biography was written in the Mid 8th Century. In 640 he became bishop of Noyon-Tournai. His diocese was full of pagans and he undertook the conversion of Frisians, Sueves, and other coastal tribes. He became the patron saint of metalworkers, especially blacksmiths and goldsmiths.

---

[193] (Tangl, Die Briefe des Heiligen Bonifatius u. Lullus 174)

Eligius Corrects the Sueves

He worked hard in Flanders. He strove ardently and continuously against Antwerp and converted many incorrect Sueves. He also ruined temples and terminated all kinds of idolatries wherever he found them.[194]

Do not let them make those images of feet, which they place in crossroads. Burn them when you find them.[195]

LIFE OF AMANDUS

Amandus died after 676. The identity of his biographer is not certain, but his biography has been attributed to Baudemund who probably wrote in the mid 8th century. In 620, Rome sent him on a Frankish mission. Amand was born to a wealthy family in Gaul. In his early life he practiced as a hermit. Later, he committed himself to missionary work among the Slavs, Basques and the people of Flanders. He visited Rome twice in his life and became a bishop in 630. Later, Rome sent Amandus on a mission to Ghent where Dagobert I supported him. He founded the monastery Elnone on the Scheldt river.

Trees and Idols

A man named Amandus was making his rounds in his diocese to care for souls when he heard tell of a village by the river Scaldus (Sheldt) that was violently ensnared in the devil's traps. The village was called Gandeus (Ghent) in ancient times. These villagers shunned God to worship trees and pieces of wood. They erected idols and temples.[196]

LIFE OF LAMBERT, BISHOP OF TRAIECTENSIS

Lambert was born in the city of Traiectensis and eventually became the bishop of the city between 670 and 675. He conducted missionary work in Toxandria to try to convert heathens. He died around 703. This biography was written in the 8th century, and its author has not been identified.

Temple Bashing

Lambert destroyed many temples and statues in Toxandria.[197]

BONIFACE

Originally named Wynfred, Saint Boniface lived from 675 to 754. He belonged to an English noble family. When he was 30, he became a Benedictine monk. In 716 he began missionary activity in Frisia. He was also active in Hesse, Thuringia and Bavaria. In

---

[194] (II, 8M.G.,Scr. rer. mer. IV 700)
[195] lib. 2 Cap. 5
[196] 13 (M.G. Scr. rer. mer. V, 436 s.)
[197] 10 (M.G., Scr. rer. Mer. VI, 363)

755 some Frisians killed him and he was later made a martyr. In 690, Willibrord left England on a mission to Frisia.

LETTER TO POPE STEPHEN

Temple Bashing
Willibrord destroyed shrines and temples. Over the course of fifty years of evangelization, he converted most of the Saxons to the Christ's faith.[198]

WILLIBALD OF MAINZ

Willibald of Mainz wrote his biography of Boniface between 755 and 768. He was an English priest who went to Germany after Boniface had died. In Germany he got a job as a canon in the church at Mainz. Willibald constructed this biography from the letters and accounts of people who had known Boniface.

Pagan Bashing in Frisia
He worked hard in Christ and won the great Frisian folk for the lord. He destroyed their springs and altars.[199]

Among the Hessians
Many Hessians converted to Catholicism and were strengthened in the seven-fold spirit's grace and accepted the laying on of hands. But some refused the documents of the pure faith. Some sacrificed secretly and others sacrificed openly in woods or springs. Some performed secret divinations, soothsaying, created illusions, and performed incantations. Some observed auguries and divinations by the flight of birds besides worshipping in all kinds of sacrificial rites. The saner minds threw away their tribal superstitions leaving them behind for good.

The Great Oak of Gasmer
He tried to cut down a huge oak tree as he had planned. It was known as the "Tree of Jupiter" in the heathens' language. It was in a place called "Gasmer."[200]

CHARLEMAGNE

Charlemagne, the Frankish king, ruled from 768 to 814. He initiated the Carolingian dynasty and the Carolingian renaissance. He fought wars against the Lombards in Italy, the Saxons in Saxony, the Bavariansin Bavaria, and the Moores in Spain. Charlemagne forcibly converted the Saxons to Christianity between 775 and 777 in numerous mass baptisms. In 800, Pope Leo III crowned him emperor.

---

[198] II, (Written in 753) (Tangl, Die Briefe des heiligen Bonifatius u. Lullus 235)
[199] 5 (ed. Levison 24)
[200] 6 (1. 1. 30 s.)

Capitularies were a form of royal edicts issued by Carolingian kings. These were not technically laws. Their authority was based on the king's right to give verbal orders, or 'bannum.'

THE FIRST CAPITULARY

Various Pagan Observances
We decree that all bishops shall carefully travel through their districts to strengthen and teach. Bishops shall do this each year, and they shall investigate and stop pagan observances, divinations, auguries by birds and lots, phylacteries, incantations, and all their filthy practices.[201]

ON THE PARTS OF SAXONY

Temples
We are all agreed that the Christian churches that we have built and consecrated to God in Saxony should have more esteem and excellence than the temples of empty idols.[202]

Cannibalism
If someone is deceived by the devil and believes and does, in accordance with the pagan customs, the following things, he shall be condemned to death. If he thinks that some man or woman is a witch (*striaga*) who eats people, and because of this, he himself cooks the flesh and gives it away for food, or, if he himself eats it, he shall be executed.[203]

Cremation
If someone cremates a dead person in a pagan rite, and reduces the bones to ashes, he gets the death penalty.[204]

Refusing Baptism
If any Saxon goes lurking unbaptized, disdaining baptism and wanting to stay pagan, kill him.[205]

Human Sacrifice
If anyone sacrifices a person to the devil and offers him in sacrifice to demons following tribal customs, he gets the death penalty.[206]

---

[201] (Shortly after 769 C.E.) 7 (M.G. Leg. Sect. II, I 45)
[202] (Written around 782.) 1 (Von Schwerin, Leges Saxonum 37)
[203] ib. 6 (1. 1. 38 s.)
[204] ib. 7 (1. 1. 38)
[205] ib. 8
[206] ib. 9 (1. 1. 39)

Groves and Springs

If a nobleman swears an oath in a spring, wood, or grove, or sacrifices anything according to the customs of his folk, he must pay 60 solidi; a freeman pays 30 and slaves pay 15.[207]

Pagan Tombs

We demand that the bodies of Christian Saxons be buried in Christian cemeteries and not in pagan tombs.[208]

Lot Casters

We decree that lot casters and diviners are to be given over to the churches and priests.[209]

HARISTALLEN'S CAPTIULARY

Oaths

Let no one presume to swear an oath secured by money in which he takes turns with others in making oaths.[210]

GENERAL ADMONITION

Storm bringers, Wizards, etc.

We decree that there are not to be any storm bringers, wizards, or oath makers. They must be corrected or condemned wherever found.[211]

Lamps at Trees and Springs

Idiots set up lamps and observe other customs at trees and springs. These are an abomination to God and shall be cast down and destroyed.

DOUBLE EDICT FOR THE LEGATIONS

Oaths

Evil drunkenness is banned entirely for everybody. We also ban oaths sworn in the name of St. Stephen made by ourselves and our sons.[212]

Ringing Bells and Pole Writings

Make sure they do not ring bells or write on poles because of hailstorms.[213]

---

[207] ib. 21 sequ. (1. c. 41)

[208] ib. 22

[209] ib. 23.

[210] (Written around 779) 16 (M.G., Leg. Sec. II, 1 51)

[211] (Written around 787) 65 (1. 1. 59)

[212] (Written around 789) 26 (1. 1. 64)

[213] ib. 34 (1. 1.)

SYNOD OF FRANKFURT

New Saints
Do not allow monuments to new saints to be erected along roads. These new saints are not be worshipped or invoked.[214]

Groves
Do not neglect your power to destroy sacred trees and groves.[215]

SPECIAL CAPITULARY

Springs Rocks and Trees
Cast down and destroy the trees, rocks and springs where idiots practice their observances.[216]

SAXON LAW

Assault
If someone charges at a person whose sword is not drawn, he shall pay twelve solidi, unless he wants a duel.[217]

COUNCIL OF NEUCHINGENSE

The council of Nuechingense was held in 772 and issued several decrees or 'decreta.'

Stapsaken
The Bavarians use the word "*Stapsaken*" and in these words we recognize an ancient and idolatrous pagan custom. In this practice they converse such that the person who has been wronged and who is owed compensation says: "You wrongfully took from me things that you should return to me. You should also pay compensation for as many solidi as it is worth." The defendant replies: "I did not take this from you, nor do I owe you compensation." The first speaker who is trying to recover his property then says: "Let us stretch our right hands to the judgment of God." Then they extend their right hands to the sky.[218]

ALCUIN OF YORK

Alcuin of York lived from around 735 to 804. He was born in York where he spent most of his life prior to moving to France to work for the Court of Charlemagne. In 778 he ran the School at York. In 782, he led the so-called 'Carolingian Renaissance' under

---

[214] (Convened in 794) c. 42 s. (1. 1. 77)

[215] ib. 43.

[216] (Promulgated in 802 C.E.) 41 (1. 1. 104)

[217] (802 or 803) 8 (Von Schwerin, Leges Saxonum 19)

[218] c. 6 (M.G., Leg. Sect. III, II, 100 s.)

Charlemagne in France. Beornrade, the Archbishop of Sens and one of Alcuin's relatives, urged him to write the Life of Willibrord which he wrote between 785 and 797.

LIFE OF WILLIBRORD

Fosites, A Sacred Spring

The pious preacher of God's word set out on his journey. On the border between the Frisians and the Danes, he came to an island called 'Fosites' after one of their Gods. Their neighbors called them 'Fosites' because their temples were constructed to this God. The Pagans worshipped here so much that nobody touched the grazing animals or anything of the kind. They are not allowed to draw water from the bubbling font, unless they do so noiselessly.

A storm once drove a man of God to this island. He stayed until the storm lifted giving him an opportunity to sail away. He witnessed the island's idiotic religion. He also saw the island's cruel king condemn violators of the spring's sacrality to terrible deaths. He invoked the trinity and baptized three men in the spring. He also planned to kill some of the island's animals for food. The pagans looked on, thinking the Christians would swiftly die or go mad. But when they saw the violators suffer no harm, they fell into a terrified bewilderment and then told King Radbod what they had seen. [219]

Burning with anger, Radbod decided to seek vengeance against the man of God for his injury against the gods and the island. He spent three days in three villages, in accordance with tradition, casting lots. But the death lot would never fall for God's servant or his companions because of God's protection. The only exception was that one man was selected by the lots to be crowned as a martyr.[220]

A Poltergeist

A horrible satanic witchery descended upon a family head and his household. The terrible occurrences and the wicked shenanigans made it clear that an evil poltergeist haunted the house. The demon would suddenly snatch up some food, clothing and other household objects and hurl them into the fire. One time it even grabbed their young son from their arms and cast him into the fire. They had much trouble . . . No priest could exorcize it.[221]

SYNOD OF BRITAIN

This is a letter by Alcuin describing a synod held in England in 786.

---

[219] 10 s. (M.G., Scr. rer. Merov. VII, 124 s.)
[220] 11.
[221] 11.

LETTERS OF ALCUIN

Piercings and Scars

We decree that all faithful Christians shall model themselves after Catholics. Cast down, remove, and disregard any pagan religious remnants. God made man fair in form and looks, yet diabolical inspiration drives the pagans to mark their bodies with the foulest scars. Prudentius says: "It stains the innocent earth with sordid blemishes." He who injures and defiles the lord's creatures would seem to injure the lord. If anyone wants this injurious disfigurement instead of God, then let him suffer severe retribution. Folks who practice their folk religion will not get health that way, any more than the Jews who are circumcised and whose hearts lack true belief.[222]

ANNALS OF THE FRANKISH KINGS

The Annals of the Frankish Kings covers the periods between 741 and 829. Its authors are unknown, but the first author probably began writing in 787 and the second and third authors probably wrote between 795 and 829. Annals of the Frankish Kings was probably written under royal patronage.

Irminsul

Then the Lord Charlemagne entered Saxony. The first thing he did was take Fort Eresburg. Then he went to Irminsul. He wrecked and looted the temple, taking all its gold and silver.[223]

PAUL THE DEACON

Paul the Deacon was born a Lombard and educated in his hometown of Friuli and at the royal Lombardic court at Pavia. In the 760's he was part of the royal Lombard Court and in the 770's Charlemagne invaded Lombardy. By 783, Paul belonged to Charlemagne's court. In 786 he studied and wrote in the monastery of Monte Cassino, where he wrote History of the Lombards. Paul the Deacon wrote this history to reconcile Lombard history with Christian history. He wrote for pedagogical purposes as well.

SONGS

Thunar and Wotan

Neither Thunar nor Wotan helped him.[224]

---

[222] 3, (M.G., Epist. IV, 26 s)
[223] DCCLXXII (rec. Kurze 32 s.)
[224] XIV, 36 (M.G., Poet. Lat. med. aev. 1, 51)

HISTORY OF THE LOMBARDS

Exile Lots

The lots dictated that this group of Lombards had to leave its homeland to seek arable land in foreign countries. They appointed as their leaders two young men, Ibor and Aion, who were much stronger and more vigorous than the other Germans. They said goodbye to their homeland and set out in search of new lands in which to live and establish settlements.[225]

The Lombard Story

They have a ridiculous fable. The Vandals went to Godan asking that he give them victory over the Winniles. Godan replied that he would give victory to whomever he saw first when the sun rose. Gambara went to Frea, the wife of Odin, and asked that the Winniles win. Frea had a plan for them. The Winnile women would loosen their hair and hang it from their faces. Then they were to go to the region where they would be seen by Godan when he looked out of his east-facing window, as he usually did in the morning. So it went. When Godan looked out at the rising sun, he said: "Who are those long beards?" Then Frea suggested that he give victory to those he had just named, and so the Winniles won.[226]

Godan, whose name is also spelled Wodan, is the same one the Romans call Mercury. He is worshipped as a God by all the German tribes. He is thought to have existed in ancient times as well in modern times.[227]

Speaking Over an Arrow

The Lombards went to Mauringa to get more warriors. They released many from slavery and gave them freedom. As was their custom, they murmured words in their language over an arrow to confirm their new status.[228]

Amazons

It is said that when the Lombards and their king were traveling they came to a river. The amazons there would not let them cross. Lamisso swam the river to have a duel with the strongest. He killed her. The Lombards praised him highly for this act, as well as getting them across the river. Both sides had reached an agreement before the duel. If the Amazon won, the Lombards leave, but if, as happened, the Amazon lost, the Lombards would be allowed to cross the river.[229]

Skala

Alboin killed Cunimund in that battle and made a drinking cup out of his head. They call this kind of cup a "skala" in their language. In Latin it is known as a "patera."[230]

---

[225] I, 3 (M.G. Scr. rer. Lang. 49)
[226] ib. 8 (1. 1. 52)
[227] ib. 9 (1. 1. 53)
[228] ib. 13 (1. 1. 54)
[229] ib. 15 (1. 1. 55)
[230] 1b. 27 (1. 1. 69)

Adultery Accusations

Queen Gundiperga, as her mother had done in Modica, had a basilica dedicated to John the Baptist built in the town of Ticenium. She had it decorated with gold, silver, and fine cloth, and had it richly endowed with other things besides. Her body was entombed in this basilica. She was accused of adultery. Her servant, Carellus, sought an audience with the king. He demanded that the accuser be brought forth so that he could prove her chastity in a duel. He met her accuser in single combat and trounced him soundly as a multitude looked on. [231]

At the Poles

"At the Poles" is what they called 'the place' because beams were once erected there in accordance with the Lombard tradition. If a Lombard died in battle or was killed in some other way, his relatives would erect a pole over his grave. At the top of the pole they fixed a wooden dove facing the place of the beloved's death. That is how they indicated the resting places of their dead. [232]

The Fly

Then King Cunincpert and his Master of Cavalry or "Maraphis" in the Lombard language, made a plan while in Ticinum town. A large fly flew in the window and landed next to them. Cunincpert tried to kill it with his knife. He managed only to chop off one of its feet.

Aldon and Grauson did not know anything about the plan and they headed for the royal palace. As they neared the martyr Romanus' basilica near the king's palace, a lame man with a foot cut off suddenly came right up to them. He told them that Cunincpert would kill them if they continued their journey. These words terrorized them and they fled to the altar in the basilica. When king Cunincpert heard that Aldon and Grauson had run into the Basilica of the holy martyr, he challenged the Maraphia accusing him of betraying their plan. The Maraphia answered saying: "My Lord King! You know that I have not left your sight since we framed this plan. How can I have revealed the plan to anyone?" The king sent a messenger to Aldon and Grauson asking why they sought refuge in the sanctuary. They replied: "Because we heard that our Lord king wants to kill us." The king sent a messenger back asking who had told them this and demanded that they reveal their source of information. He told them they could not return to his good graces if they would not tell. They told the king that a lamer came up to them and that one of his feet was missing and replaced by some sort of wooden foot. This was the man who had warned them of the doom that awaited them. The king realized that the fly whose foot he amputated was an evil spirit and that it had revealed the secret plan. [233]

---

[231] IV, 45 (1. 1. 136)
[232] ib. V, 34 (1. 1. 156)
[233] ib.VI, 6 (1. 1. 168)

The Cuckoo
When they handed the staff to Hildebrand, as was traditional, a cuckoo bird flew towards the staff and landed on it. To some wise persons this seemed a portent of things to come and to signify that his rule would be ineffectual.[234]

PSEUDO BONIFACE

This sermon has been attributed to Boniface of Mainz, who died around 754 but this document seems to have been written around 800.

Sermon: (On Various Pagan Gods and practices)

The following are capital offences: Sacrilegious veneration of idols and all pagan auguries and sacrifices, including sacrifices to dead bodies or over sepulchers. Auguries, phylacteries, and sacrifices made over rocks, at springs and trees are also sacrilegious. Also bad are sacrifices made to Jupiter, Mercury or any other Pagan Gods, since these are all demons. There are many other such practices, but it would take too long to enumerate them here.[235]

LIFE OF WULFRAM

The Merovingian bishop and missionary, Wulfram, died around 694. Wulfram became bishop of Sens in 682 and left this post to convert Frisians. An unknown biographer wrote this life circa 800.

King Radbod
When they had gotten everything together that seemed necessary for the voyage, they went to the monastery port and boarded the boat. They sailed through the great river of the Sequannae into the Gallic Sea and sailed into Frisia. He went to preach the word of God to the Frisian leader, Radbod. They told him that things that men make with their hands are not gods. He told him that you couldn't make a God out of stone or wood as these materials could be cut or burned. He also said that mortals can reshape these into all kinds of other utilitarian objects or can be despised and tossed down to be trampled under foot and turned back into earth. God's eternal throne is not to be found in cheap and transitory metal, but in the heavens. . . . He was freely heard at the assemblies and he baptized many among the weak and the noble alike everyday and they were absolved of idolatry at the font of faith. The above-mentioned leader did not prohibit this and the word was heard by those who would listen. Radbod's own son was among them. He believed and was baptized.[236]

One day, when he was preaching and teaching among the Frisians, he met a young Frisian boy whom the duke was leading to the gallows to be sacrificed to the gods. The

---

[234] ib. 55 (1. 1. 184)
[235] VI, I (Migne, P. L. LXXXIX, 855)
[236] 4 (M.G., Scr. rer. Mer. V 664)

holy priest asked the duke not to sacrifice humans to bad demons. He asked the duke to spare the boy and that he be allowed to take care of the boy. The boy was named Ovo. Radbod answered in Frisian saying that in days of yore their predecessors required that human sacrifices be chosen by lot and had established the eternal law. . . . The boy hung for two hours before a crowd of spectators that included both Christians and kinsmen.[237]

There were two more Frisian lads who were likewise to be sacrificed to demons . . . The previously mentioned leader, Radbod, brought the unbelievers a custom devised by the devil that involved sacrificing humans to gods that were really just demons. This was done at religious rites by various methods. By demonic inspiration, some were killed in gladiatorial combats, some hung in fork shaped gibbets, some were hung with nooses, and some were submerged in the brackish waters. This tribe chose to sacrifice a widow and her two dear children in the depths of the sea. They were enclosed in a place where the tide came in and the waves swallowed them. It was terrible. It is said they do this every seven years.[238]

Radbod Prefers his Ancestors and Family to Heaven

King Radbod was about to get baptized. He stepped back from the holy bishop Wulfram, refraining from swearing his oaths in the name of God. He wanted to know whether most of the Frisian kings, princes and nobles would definitely dwell in that celestial region in which he expected he would dwell, if he believed and was baptized, or whether they would dwell in that place Wulfram had called the damned Tartarus. Blessed Wulfram said: "Make no mistake, famous prince, the chosen are with God. But your ancestors, the leaders of the Frisian folk, who departed without the sacrament of baptism, definitely received the sentence of damnation. But whoever will believe and be baptized will enjoy eternal joy with Christ." King Radbod heard this as he was walking toward the font. But as he neared the font, he stepped back. He said that he could not leave the company of his ancestors, the Frisian leaders, to reside in that celestial kingdom with a puny pack of paupers.[239]

LIFE OF BARBATUS

Barbatus became bishop of Benevento in 663 and he died in 683. He was an ardent pagan basher. His biography was written no earlier than the 9th century.

The viper cult was native to Beneventum from classical times. We are not given enough details here to guess at how much of the Lombard practice was classically based and how much of their own religion may have intermingled with Roman practices. Snakes and dragons have been a primary subject of art and myth among the Germans, but we have little evidence that they were worshipped. In Germany, snakes appear to have had more positive symbolism than that which has come down to us through Scandinavian literature. In Widukind's story of Hathagat, a dragon on a battle standard symbolizes one of the virtues.

---

[237] 6 (1. 1. 665)
[238] 8 (1. 1. 667)
[239] 9. (1. 1. 668)

Dragons and serpents were one the chief Germanic ornamental motifs and likely adorned most Germanic temples.

Viper Cult and Votum
The Lombards clung to an old folk-rite in those days, even though they had been baptized. Their beastly minds made and worshipped an image of an animal commonly known as a viper. They bowed their heads before this, when they should have bent before the creator for their debt. In a yearly ritual they worshipped a tree as if it were sacred. This was not far from Benevenutem's walls. They would hang a hide from the tree and gather around it. Then they would turn around and ride swiftly away, driving their horses with their spurs trying to outrace one another. In mid-course, they would turn and throw javelins back at the hide. Each would then take a piece of the hide and superstitiously swear stupid oaths. Because of this they called this place "votum" . . . [240]

Chopping Down Votum
Blessed Barbatus suddenly grabbed up an axe. He strode up to "Votum" and chopped down the loathsome tree with his own hands. He covered the area with earth so that no one would know where it had stood.[241]

Romvault and his associates stayed blinded by their traditional error, even though the all-powerful God had saved them from the traps of their enemies. God's servants got this done by praying. In public they professed allegiance to Barbatus' God, but when out of public view, they worshipped their viper statue. . . .

Romvoult's wife, Theodora, entirely rejected her husband's error and worshipped Jesus Christ in accordance with the holy canons. Barbatus, God's man, would visit her with her approval while Romvault went hunting. Barbatus started talking to her about her man's cowardice. She drew a deep breath and said: "If only you would pray to All Powerful God. I know that God will stop him and make him walk the truth road, if you intervene." Barbatus told her: "If you really trust in God, and I think you do, then fear not, and listen to my plan. Bring me the viper statue and your husband will be saved."

She had considerable faith in God's man and eagerly brought him the statue. Barbatus looked at it and then melted it down in a fire. He brought a number of goldsmiths. They beat the gold into a chalice and an offering dish for the body and blood of Christ. These vessels were marvelous for their size and beauty. They crafted them before the king's return. Thus the monument was preserved for the future in the Blessed Mother's church. They were saved inwardly and outwardly from the enemy by this act.[242]

---

[240] I (M.G. Scr. rer. Lang. 557)
[241] 7 (1. 1. 560)
[242] 8 (1. 1. 561)

EXCERPTS FROM THE GALLIC HISTORY

The author of this work is unknown. This history was probably written in the 8ᵗʰ or 9ᵗʰ centuries and perhaps even up to, but not after, 1064.

The Goddess Cizae

After this happened near the Rhine, the Roman People suffered a grievous blow on the borders of Noricum. The German tribes occupying Rhetia were not far from the Alps. They were a like distance from the open fields where the two swiftest rivers flow together. In Noricum's borderlands stands a city with a rampart and a ditch instead of walls. They named this city 'Cizerim' after the Goddess Cizae, whom they worshipped with the utmost reverence. Her temple was made of wood in accordance with the barbarian religious traditions. It remained unharmed, even after the fall of the Roman colony. After the temple was gone, the hill kept the goddess' name.

Here, on August 1, the praetor, Titus Annius, had his army build walls around the city to defend against the barbarian invasions. At the southern part of the city, his most industrious legion fortified camp Mars. Avar, the son of king Bogudis sat to the west. He had crossed the river and encamped between the river and the ramparts with the entire cavalry and the Macedonian auxiliaries. This was an unfortunate accident since there was not enough room for a camp. But they were well drilled in both Greek and Roman military styles.

Fifty-nine days after this, the barbarians held a well-attended festival in goddess Cizae's honor. It was more of a jovial party than a serious affair.

Suddenly, he burst from the nearby woods and with a great throng of barbarians, overrunning the cavalry. What is worse, he routed the allied auxiliaries. When the enemies took Avar alive in his royal garb, they sacrificed him like a cow. But what do the barbarians know about religion?[243]

THE BRIEF LAURISSEN CHRONICLE

Very little is known of this obscure chronicle, which was probably written around 806.

Irminsul

Charlemagne assaulted Fort Eresburg in Saxony and destroyed their famous holy grove known as Irminsul.[244]

---

[243] (M.G., Scr. XXIII, 338 s.)

[244] Clemens, Carolus, 54; and IV, 3 (ed. Schnorr von Carlsfield, Nues Archiv der Gesellschaft für Altere Deutsche Geschichtkunde 36, 1911, 30)

WETTINUS

The monk, hagiographer and schoolmaster, Wettinus, wrote a <u>Life of Gallus</u> between 816 and 824 C.E in Reichenau. The Irish monk, Gallus, went with Columbanus from Ireland to the continent for missionary work among the Brigantes. He probably died around 650.

LIFE OF GALLUS

Bronze and Gold Bulls

Columbanus, God's man, boarded a ship with his best disciple, Gallus, and another deacon. They went to the town of Brigantia to look around. . . . That tribe worshipped three bronze and gold images in accordance with their folkish religious traditions. They thought they should pray to these instead the world's creator. . . .There was a folkmoot at the temple in a customary festival. But this was more a spectacle for strangers than true reverence or devotion.[245]

Demons

Gallus, chosen by God, cast his net into the water in the still of the night. He heard a sudden shout from the mountaintop. It came from a demon shouting at another demon in the water. The demon in the water shouted to the other "I am over here!" The one on the mountain yelled: "Help me! Look! The wanderers who drove me from my temple are coming. They are destroying the gods worshipped by the natives and converting them to the worship of their own God. Come! Come! Help me drive them from the land!" The demon in the sea shouted: "One of them is in the sea, but I can never harm him. I want to break his net, look! Faith has beaten me. The standard prayer always wards him and he never sleeps."[246]

EIGIL

Eigil, the Abbot of Fulda from 818 to 822, died in 822. Eigil probably wrote his <u>Life of Sturmus</u> between 794 and 800. Sturmus was the abbot of Fulda from 744 to his death in 779.

LIFE OF STURMUS

Charles had ruled beneficently for four years. The Saxons, a savage and dangerous tribe, was known to celebrate pagan rites. King Charles was very Christian and always devoted to the Lord. He started thinking about how he might win the Saxons for Christ. . . . Sturmus gave pastoral care to most of each folk. He worked during this advantageous time to teach them the holy word so that they would abandon idols and statues, support the faith of Christ, destroy temples, and build holy basilicas.[247]

---

[245] 6 (MG Scr. rer. Mer. IV, 260)
[246] ib. 7 (1. 1. 261)
[247] 22 MG Scr. II 376

EINHARD

Einhard was born in France near Main in 775 and raised in the Monastery at Fulda. He became part of Charlemagne's court in 791. Einhard founded the palace school that Alcuin led. Einhard wrote <u>Life of Charlemagne</u> between 817 and 836.

Life of Charlemagne

Heroic Poetry
Then Charlemagne also had committed to writing for the benefit of future generations the antique and barbaric songs that extol the heroic deeds of ancient kings.

<u>NENNIUS</u>

Nennius was a welsh historian who wrote his <u>British History</u> between 796 and 830. This is the oldest source of Arthurian lore.

BRITISH HISTORY

Hengist and Horsa
Roman rule disappeared from Britain and the British lived in fear for forty years. Vortigern ruled in Britain and was stressed by his fear of the Picts, the Scotts, Roman invasion, and especially Ambrose. Then three ships came, full of exiles from Germany. The brothers Hengist and Horsa were aboard. They were the sons of Wictgils, son of Witta, son of Wechta, son of Woden, son of Frealaf, Son of Fredulf, son of Finn, son of Foscwald, son of Geta, whom they say was the son of God. This is not the God of Gods himself, amen, the Lord of Hosts, but just one of the idols they worshipped.[248]

ERMOLDUS NIGELLUS

Ermold Nigellus lived from around 790 to 838. He wrote <u>In Honor of Ludovick</u> between 826 and 827 to regain the favor of the royal family which had confined him to Strasbourg in 824. It worked. He returned to the royal court under Pepin I in 824.

IN HONOR OF LUDOVICK

Horse's Whinny
He was soon traveling the road in night's welcome silence. Regrettably, his horse whinnied too loudly and the guards roused the army in the camp and they soon discovered the source of the whinny and went after it.[249]

---

[248] 31 (M.G. Auct. Ant. XII, 170 s.)
[249] I, 451 s. (MG Poet. Lat. II, 19)

A Sneaky Snake

The Danes were a tribe that revered a sneaky snake. This was back in the old days. Barbatus exposed this evil and preached God to those heathens, for they celebrated ancient and wicked religious rites. So also did he bring the word of Christ to the heathens who worshipped empty idols and also Neptune in the stead of the creator. Jupiter was the highest and they thought he was very holy indeed.[250]

Metal Statues

It is good to abandon worthless things. To venerate metal statues is a criminal act for humans. This raises questions as to the usefulness of Jupiter, Neptune, other Gods, and metal statues made by human hands.[251]

Jupiter

The terrible monster is far away and Jupiter is gone. He left Jupiter and now reveres the church.[252]

Praying for Prosperity

I always sacrificed as a suppliant to my Gods and Goddesses. I would piously pray that they would serve and bless the ancestral kingdom with all its people, property and their hearths. I prayed that the Gods would drive out famine and other vile things while bringing prosperity to my people.[253]

PENITENTIAL OF THE PSEUDO THEODORE

Falsely attributed to Theodore of Tarsus, this penitential was probably written between 830 and 847. It draws heavily from the genuine Penitential of Theodore and a penitential by Cummean. Thorpe published it as the genuine Penitential of Theodore in his Ancient Laws of England.

Closing a Hole With Thorns

Should a man pass through a hole in the earth for his son's health, and afterwards close it with thorns, let him pay penance by living on bread and water for sixty days.[254]

LIFE OF WILLIHAD

The English missionary to Frisia and Bremen, Willehad, lived from around 735 to 789. In 765 he worked in Frisia and in 780 began work in the lower Weser region. He became bishop of Bremen. His biography was written between 838 and 860 in Echternach. The author of the biography is unknown. Another work, The Miracles of Willehad, was written by Ansgar.

---

[250] ib. IV, 5 s. (1. 1. 59)

[251] ib. 67 s. (1. c. 60)

[252] ib. 99 s. (1. 1. 61)

[253] ib. 311 (1. 1. 67)

[254] Clemens, Carolus Fontes Historiae Religionis Germanicae, 1928, p. 56. C. XII (27), 16 (Wassersbleben, Bussordnungen 597)

Idol Worship
Dockychira left and crossed the river Loveke and then arrived at a place called Humarcha. He started preaching about God to the barbarians there. He had them forsaking superstitious idol worship and coming around to the idea of one true God. They came to believe that they could cleanse their hearts by baptism.

Rocks
He told them it was stupid and useless to try to get any help from a rock, or to get any comfort or sanctuary from statues that do not speak or listen. When the wild folks heard this, they were given over to idolatry in a big way. His words whipped them into such a fury that they began making high-pitched whistling noises through their teeth. They shouted that such a blasphemer should die for using his eloquence to profane their unconquerable Gods.

Lots
Nevertheless, he did convince some of them by adopting a more reasonable plan. They suggested that since this religion was unknown to them they should cast lots to find out if he should die or if he was worthy of heaven. They argued that he should go free if not guilty of any crimes and not be executed as if he had killed a kinsman. They were persuaded and cast lots in accordance with their folkish customs to decide whether he would live or die.[255]

Temple Bashing
Thus divine ardor smote those same disciples and they started wrecking temples that the folk had built in accordance with its customs.[256]

THE ANCIENT LIFE OF LEBUIN

Lebuin was an English Benedictine monk who lived in the 8th Century. He accompanied Boniface and numerous other monks on a mission to the pagans of Germany. Lebuin tried to convert Saxons and Franks in the Vicinity of the river Ysel. In 754 he went with Marchelm, a disciple of Willibrord, to preach to the Frisians. The author of this life is unknown, but it was probably written between 840 and 864. It was used as source material for a later life by Hucbald of St. Amand around 900.

Yearly Moot
The ancient Saxons did not have kings but rather established regional leaders. Their custom was to hold a general council yearly. It is held in central Saxony by a river at a place called Marklo.[257]

---

[255] 3 (Acta Sanctorum Nov. III, 843)
[256] ib. 4 (1. 1.)
[257] 4s. (M.G. Scr. XXX, 2 793)

All the satraps were present who were supposed to be when the day of the general council came. They all gathered together and performed a supplication rite to their highest gods. They prayed for the protection of their fatherland. They intended to please all the Gods in this convention, etc.[258]

ALTFRID

Altfrid of Munster was bishop of Munster from 839 to his death in 849. He wrote the biography of Ludger (also spelled Liudger), who may have been his nephew. The Frisian Saint Ludger lived from 744 to 809. He became the bishop of Munster in 804. He was active also in the Saxon church and helped to establish a monastery in Ruhr. He was involved in missionary activity among the Frisians and Saxons.

LIFE OF ST. LUDGER

At the time of his birth, Liafburg had a pagan grandmother who completely left the Catholic religion. She, whose name we will not mention, got mad at Liafburg's wife because she bore him many daughters, but no living sons. He ordered his attendants to grab the child away from her mother and kill her before she could suck any of her mother's milk. It was the heathen custom not to kill an infant son or daughter after the infant had eaten any earthly food.[259]

Merciful God caused a neighbor lady to pity the child. The woman grabbed the child away from the hands of the henchmen and ran to the house with her. She slammed the door behind her and dashed into the bedroom where she found some honey. She put some honey in the child's mouth. The child swallowed the honey.[260]

The executioners soon arrived to execute the lady's orders. The mistress stormed about her son's house. She picked up the child and carried her to the henchmen to show them that the child was licking its lips. Their folk custom prevented them from killing her.

Temple Busting

After this, Albricius sent Ludger and other servants of God to wreck the temples and other places where the Frisians worshipped idols. They hauled back a hoard of treasure taken from the temples. Charlemagne, the ruler, took two thirds of it and gave the third part to Albricius for his personal use.[261]

Saxons Go Back to Heathenism

Ludger, God's man, stayed there for seven years because he loved teaching so much. Widukind rose to leadership among the heathen Saxons. He turned the Frisians away from God, burned churches, and drove God's servants to the river Fleo. After causing the

---

[258] ib. 6.
[259] Clemens, p. 58; and 1, 6 s (ed. Diekampt, Geschichtsquellendes Bistums Munster IV, 10 s.)
[260] ib. 7.
[261] ib. 16 (1. 1. 20)

Frisians to drop Christianity, he soon had them sacrificing to idols and practicing erroneous ancient customs.[262]

Foseta
Ludger went into Frisian and Dane country and then to an island they call Fosetland after one of their false gods. . . . He crossed over to the island and destroyed the temples built in Foseta's honor. He built a church there in its stead. He gorged the natives on Christianity and baptized them in the spring while invoking the trinity. This deed gladdened him because Willibrord once baptized three men in a spring in which no one dared drink unless silently.[263]

THE PASSION OF KILIAN, MARTYR OF WIRZBURG

Saint Kilian was born in 640 in Ireland and died around 689. He became the bishop of Wurzburg and worked to convert Thuringia, for which he was eventually killed and made a martyr. His life was written in the mid 9th Century.

Cane the Fool
An eloquent man readied a reply to unhappy Geliana's suggestion to her husband. She had said "Think of yourself and the rest of us whom they will baptize all at the same time when deciding whether their God is really all powerful. Think of this when you are trying to find out whether his god is really omniscient and repays good for good and evil for evil to folks who do not correct themselves and pay penance. Why not unchain the fool. Have the people judge him. If his God is like he says, then cane the man and let that God strive mightily to protect his servants."

"If it turns out his God is not so great, then let me speak in behalf of Diana to keep her from getting mad. We want to serve Diana, just as our ancestors did, for they were well off up until now." [264]

FRISIAN LAW

Compiled after 850, this code contains 22 titles and the Addition of the Wise contains another 12 titles.

Oaths on Relics, Money and Clothing
A slave accused of stealing anything valuable, or of serious bodily injury, shall swear to his lord on saints' relics. A slave accused of a minor robbery or injury shall swear over clothing or money.[265]

---

[262] ib. 21 (1. 1. 24 s.)
[263] ib. 22 (1. 1. 26 s.)
[264] 13 (MG., Scr. rer. mer. V, 727)
[265] XII (M.G. Leg. Tom. III, 666)

69

ADDITION OF THE WISE

Stealing from Temples
Someone breaking into a temple and stealing sacred things is to be led to sea and onto the sand that is covered by water when the tide is in. His ears are to be slit, he is to be castrated, and then sacrificed to the Gods whose temple he violated.[266]

Dueling
In this combat, each side can pick a champion to fight in his place, if he can find one. . . [267]

HINCMAR OF REIMS

Hincmar, Archbishop from 845 to 822, was born in 806 and died in 882. He served as an advisor to King Louis the Pious starting in 834 and again for Charles the Bald in 840. He was a champion of the resistance of the French church to papal authority, and opposed the idea of papal supremacy. He was also actively reorganizing his diocese and thereby gained the enmity of various secular and ecclesiastical authorities. In the synod of Soissons he defended himself for such actions as nullifying ordinations of clergy made by the prior archbishop. He wrote capitula addressing the behavior of the clergy, among other things. The following passage indicates that some of the clergy knew how to have a good time.

SYNODIC CAPITULA

Bears and Dancing Girls
No presbyters shall gather for the 33rd or 7th anniversary of any dead people. Nor shall they drink at meetings. None shall pray to a saint's love or toast his spirit. None shall gather others for drinking, foreign prayers, inappropriate laughing, or clapping. Do not allow anyone to tell obscene jokes, sing idle fables, or bring on the bears or dancing girls. Nor shall they conspire to bring out masks of those demons called 'Talamascas' since this is diabolical and forbidden by the sacred canons.[268]

RUDOLPH, MONK OF FULDA

Rudolph, the monk and chronicler at Fulda, died in 865 C.E. He was a student of Rabanus Maurus at the monastery at Fulda. He began writing the Translation of Alexander in 863 at the request of one of Widukind's grandsons, Waltbrat. The work had to be completed by Meginhart.

---

[266] XI (1. 1. 696 s.)
[267] ib. XIV, 7 (1. 1. 668)
[268] 14 (Migne, PL CXXV, 776)

TRANSLATION OF SAINT ALEXANDER

Paraphrasing Tacitus

The Saxons worship those who are not gods by nature. They especially revere Mercury. They customarily sacrifice humans to Mercury on certain days. They think it unfitting to their Gods' greatness and worth to house them in temples or to depict them in human alikeness. Instead, they hallow woods and groves in the names of their Gods and visit these solitary places alone and with reverence. They are much given to lots and auguries. Their lot casting method is simple. They cut off a slender green branch from a fruit-bearing tree and cut this into tines. These tines are marked with certain symbols and strewn randomly over a white cloth. The caster lifts each tine three times looking up to the sky and praying to the gods. He then interprets them according to symbols carved into them. Further inquiries are made if the lots allow. If the lots do not allow it, then no further castings are done that day.

They also divine by the whinnies of a certain type of horses. This is a tribal custom. They get premonitions and forewarnings from their horses' whinnies and frothings. The nobles heed these signs as much as the commoners.

When a big war breaks out, they capture an enemy and pit him in a duel against a warrior from their own tribe. Both combatants wear the armor of their respective tribes. The outcome is taken as a portent. Certain days are also thought portentous. They believe that the new and full moon are auspicious for the initiating business dealings. They are ensnared in many other vain superstitions, but I will pass over these. [269]

Irminsul

They also exhibit reverence for the leafy trees and springs. They worship as divine a very tall tree trunk that they have erected. They call it 'Irminsul' in their own language. In Latin it is called the 'Universal Column' as if it supported everything. [270]

RIMBERT

Rimbert, the second archbishop of Bremen, lived until around 888. He succeeded Ansgar, the first archbishop of Bremen. He met Ansgar as a young monk at Turholt. Rimbert went on missions to the North and preached among the Swedes as Ansgar himself had done. He wrote his Life of Ansgar between 865 and 876. Ansgar died unmartyred in 865, but became a saint nevertheless.

---

[269] 2 (MG SCR II, 675)
[270] ib. 3 (1. 1. 676)

LIFE OF ANSKAR

Sacrifices

Heriger, the governor of Birka was not there with the businessmen and others who were staying there. They got in a jam and asked the neighboring town for help. They started sacrificing and praying to their Gods, who are really demons. They hoped to get help from them as they were in great danger. . . . There was no hope that it would go away because they kept on encouraging one another to make bigger offerings and greater oaths to their gods. Heriger, who was faithful to the Lord, got mad and railed at them: "Those vows and sacrifices you make to your idols are witchcraft. For how long will you return to poverty and destruction with your empty vows. Look at how much you have given and how much you promise. You have given one hundred pounds of silver so far and what good has it done you?"[271]

Idol Worship

Many Christians in Sliavich had been baptized in Dorstadt or Hamburg. They got more respect than anyone else in the village. They were glad for a chance to exercise their Christianity. There are many other examples of men and women who abandoned superstitious idol worship and converted to Christianity.[272]

A Mortal at a God Moot

He sailed the sea for twenty days until he got to Birka, where he found the king and a major part of the population confused by erroneous ways. The devil knew the holy man was coming so he contrived to have a man appear to the people. This man claimed to have just attended a council of the Gods and that he bore a message from the gods for the king and the people. It went like this: "We have favored you and you have resided long in this land. By our help, you have had peace and prosperity. You have sworn and sacrificed to us. But now you are withdrawing from customary sacrifices and vows and are slow to make offerings. To regain our favor, increase the offerings you have not been making and swear stronger vows. Stop worshipping that foreign God whose teachings are hostile to us. If you do not have enough Gods, and you want more, we unanimously accept your king Eric into our company and he may be numbered among us."

This bad message was announced officially in public, and by the time the bishop arrived, it had confused the minds of the whole folk. This error confused men's hearts most effectively. They stood before a temple to the aforementioned king. They had just started offering sacrifices and making oaths to him as if he were a God. The Lord bishop arrived and began asking friends there what the king was doing to stop all this. . . . He became anxious and formed a plan to invite the king to his lodgings. . . . He responded to the bishop's words joyfully and gratefully. He said. "We have had clerics here before, but it was popular sedition rather than a royal order that drove them away. Therefore, I dare not do anything before I consult our Gods by means of lots."[273]

[271] Clemens p. 61-62; L 19 (rec. Waitz 42)
[272] ib. 24 (1. 1. 52 s.)
[273] ib. 26 (1. 1. 56 s)

Lots

They went into the field in accordance with their tradition and cast lots. The lots failed because the will of God had established the Christian religion here.[274]

Finally, on the ninth day, the Sueves tired of the long bloodbath. They panicked and their timid hearts thought only of escape. . . . Then they were no longer confused and they knew not what to do. They quit using lots to find out whether their Gods wanted to help them, or to find out whether they would win or escape alive. They cast aside their lots because they could not find a God who could help them.[275]

NOTKER THE STAMMERER

The poet and chronicler, Notker Balbulus, lived from around 840 to 912. He joined the Benedictine monastery in Sankt Gallen in Switzerland when a boy and later became a teacher and librarian there and wrote Deeds of Charlemagne *in 833. This work is full of the sort of folkish stories exemplified by the following passage.*

DEEDS OF CHARLEMAGNE

A Troll

In ancient Frankland there was another bishop who was quite miserly. Barrenness devastated the whole land in an unusual year. A greedy businessman was gladdened by the people's need, as they were near to dying. He charged them exorbitant prices for his goods.

Along came a troll that made a hobby of tricking and deluding people. The troll started visiting a blacksmith's house where it stayed up at night playing with the smith's hammers and anvils. The father tried to protect his household by making the sign of the health giving cross.

The hairy troll said to him: "Let me play around in your shop and you will find your cup full each day." This wretch feared hunger more than the eternal damnation of his soul, so he agreed. The troll broke into the cellar quite a number of times. The troll hauled in a large cask and stole as much of the smith's Bacchus or Dis as it wanted. He spilled the rest on the floor.

The bishop noticed what was going on after several barrels had been drained, and considered the possibility that some malarkey might be afoot. He sprinkled holy water around the cellar and made the sign of the cross. The troll came back at night hauling a big cask. But he did not dare touch the wine barrels because the sign of the cross was protecting them. He could not even find his way out. The family security guard found

---

[274] ib. 27 (1. 1. 58)
[275] ib. 30 (1. 1. 61)

73

him in human form and tied him up. The troll was brought before the folk, tried as a thief and executed. He shouted: "Damn! I lost my friend's drinking cup."[276]

THE GERMAN CHURCH CORRECTOR'S PENITENTIAL

This was probably written in the early 11th century, though another view is that it was written as early as the 10th century. There is some overlap between these rules and those of Burchard.

Hulda
Have you believed that there is a certain woman who is able to do this thing which folks deluded by the devil say that they have to do by necessity or by the devil's command: with a throng of demons transformed into the likeness of a woman, the witch (*striga*) that the stupidity of the commoners calls Hulda, has to ride on certain nights in the guise of a woman on certain beasts in whose fellowship she has been numbered. Do you believe this?[277]

Knots, Grain, Wagons and Carding Combs
Did you pass your young son or daughter over a bier or an oven for their health? Did you burn grain by a dead person? Did you tie a belt into knots to hurt someone? Did you ever clap together the wool carding combs used by young women over a dead body? Did you ever divide a wagon in two and then carry a dead body out of the house and then go between the two wagon halves?[278]

Water by a Grave
Have you done, or allowed to be done, those things that idiotic women often do? When a man's dead body lies in the house they run to the water and secretly draw the water with a dish and then put it out into the bier. When they take the body out of the house they are careful not to raise it above knee level, thinking this is good for healing.[279]

Salve for a Dead Man's Wounds
Did you either do, or allow to be done, those things often done for the burial of the slain. They put unguent in the deceased's hands and bury him with it as if this unguent will heal wounds after death?[280]

Jumping Barley Corn
Many do the following; do you? They scrape their fireplace and set barleycorns there. If the grain jumps, they think danger is imminent, but if the grain lies still, they think that all will be well.[281]

---

[276] I, (ed. Meyer von Kronau 20 s.)
[277] Clemens p. 64: c. 70 (Schmitz, Bussbucher II, 425)
[278] c. 95 (1. 1. 430)
[279] c. 96 (1. 1.)
[280] c. 97 (1. 1. 431)
[281] c. 101 (1. 1. 435)

Looking under Rocks

Did you do what some do when they visit someone who is sick? When they approach the house where the sick person lies, they turn a stone and look in the place where the stone lay to see if anything lived under it. If they find moss or a worm or an ant or anything that moves, they are assured that the sick person will recover? If they find nothing that moves, then they think the person will die.[282]

Small Bows for Trolls

Have you made small bows and shoes sized for small boys and placed them in your cellar or barn for satyrs and trolls (pilosi) so that they will bring good things that belong to others and make you richer.[283]

Croaking Crows

Some have beliefs about beginning journeys, do you? They think that their trip will be rewarding if a crow croaks at them from their left. If they are looking for a place to stay at night, they seek an omen from a bird known as a 'mouse catcher.' They look to see if a 'mouse catcher' catches mice, eats them, and then flies in front of them and across the road they are on. They heed these auguries more than God.[284]

Rooster Crow

Do you believe this thing which some believe? They think that if they need to go out before light, they dare not depart before cockcrow. They think that after the rooster crows there is less danger. They think the rooster has the power to drive away evil spirits or to calm the spirits with his song. They think this more powerful than the human mind when inspired by the faith or the cross.[285]

Fates and the Werewolf

Many believe this, do you? Some think that those commonly known as the 'fates' (*parcae*) have special powers. When a man is born, they have the power to designate for him what they please, and can give a man the power to transform himself into a wolf, which is called a werewolf (*werewulff*) in Teutonic.[286]

Forest Maidens

Many believe this; do you also believe that certain rural women called *Sylvaticae* are able to take a corporal form when they want to appear to their lovers, and after they have been delighted with them, fade away and disappear?[287]

Setting a Place for the Fates

Did you do as certain women do during a certain time of the year? Did you set two tables and fix two meals in your house? Did you put a drink on the table along with three

---

[282] c. 102 (1. 1. 435)
[283] c. 103 (1. 1.)
[284] c. 149 (1. 1. 441 s.)
[285] c. 150 (1. 1. 442)
[286] c. 151 (1. 1.)
[287] c. 152 (1. 1.)

knives in case the 'three sisters' arrive? Previous generations called them the 'fates' (*parcae*) out of ignorance. Did you do these things so that the fates could be refreshed? Did you take away the power of divine piety and give it to the devil so that he and the sisters could help you now or in the future?[288]

Hamramr

Do you believe what women converted back to Satan believe? Do you affirm the truth of the notion that when you go to bed and you lie with your lover that you can, if you want, go about in a corporal form through closed doors and wander about the land with others deluded by the same error? So you think that you can kill with invisible weapons Christian men who have been redeemed by the blood of Christ. Do you think that you can eat their boiled flesh and then put straw or wood or anything else in place of his heart to bring him to life again and give him a new lease on life?[289]

Do you believe, as certain women do? Do you think that you can rise in the silence of the night with other associates of the devil and go through closed doors, into the sky and up into the clouds? Do you believe that you can there have duels with others such that those wounded in such battles will have actual wounds?[290]

Carrying a Child Through a Hole in the Ground

Have you done what certain women have done? When their babies cry they sometimes try to stop the crying by digging a hole in the ground and carrying the child through the hole.[291]

Infants who Die Unbaptized

Have you been driven by the same diabolical impulse as certain other women have? When an infant dies unbaptized, these women carry it away to a certain secret place where they transfix it with a pole. They say that if they do not do this, the infant will rise and harm many people.[292]

Stake in the Heart

Did you do as some are accustomed to do when they are filled with demonic audacity? When a woman dies in childbirth they transfix the mother and the child with a pole in the same grave.[293]

PENITENTIAL OF ARUNDEL

Little is known about this penitential, but it was probably written around the 10th or 11th century.

---

[288] c. 153 (1. 1. 443)
[289] c. 170. (1. 1. 446)
[290] c. 171 (1. 1. 446)
[291] c. 179 (1. 1. 448)
[292] c. 180 (1. 1.)
[293] c. 181 (1. 1.)

Black Magic

Those who are judged guilty of black magic by means of fights, boiling water, hot iron, cold water, or any other legitimate means, shall cast off their evil by doing penance for three years for the more serious offenses and two years for minor offenses.[294]

Fate Tables

Those who prepare a table for the fates should do penance for two years.[295]

Levitation

If someone thinks himself to have been raised into the air by wicked women, let him do penance for two years.[296]

Necromancy

If someone inquires into the future by going to sepulchers or grave mounds or by sacrificing to demons, they shall do 15 years of penance if done voluntarily, or 7 years if they did it because they were compelled by fear or by some enemy's force. If deacons, bishops or presbyters lapse into this crime, they shall leave their office and perform the prescribed penitence, but they will not lose their rank.[297]

LAWS OF ETHELSTAN

The English King, Ethelstan, issued these laws somewhere between 925 and 939.

False Oaths

If someone swears a false oath and it is becomes clear that he has lied, he shall not be buried in any sanctified burial ground.[298]

WIDUKIND OF CORVEY

Widukind was a monk in the monastery of Corvey. He composed his History in the time of Otto the Great, probably between 967 and 970. Deeds of the Saxons gives considerable attention to Otto and some scholars think Widukind to have been a member of Otto's court.

DEEDS OF SAXONS

Hathegat

In the same camp was a certain man among the veterans who was very old, but thriving in a vigorous old age. They said he was a grandfather whose sons were noble and manly. His name was Hathegat.

---

[294] c. 78 (Schmitz, Bussbucher I, 457)
[295] c. 83 (1. 1. 460)
[296] c. 84 (ib.)
[297] c. 88 (1. 1. 461)
[298] I. 26

A Battle Standard

Hathegat seized the battle standard, which the Saxons held sacred. It displayed an image of a lion and a dragon, with an eagle flying from above. By this he would show the effectiveness of their bravery, wisdom and other such virtues. The activity of his body showed the constancy of his mind. He spoke saying: "So far I have lived among the best Saxons, and life has led me to this old age, practically the end of my life. I have never seen my Saxons flee. And how should I now want to do a thing I have never learned to do? I know for sure that I neither know how, nor want, to run away. If the fates do not allow me to live beyond this, then so be it. To die among my friends is such a sweet thing. The bodies of friends who lie slain around us are to me examples of ancestral virtue to me. They preferred to die than be conquered; they preferred to lose their energetic spirits (lives) than to yield the field facing enemies. But why do I bother reminding you even for a moment of contempt for death? Look! We are going safely to a massive slaughter, not to a fight. Because of a promise of peace, and our big disaster, they suspect nothing; and they are so exhausted by today's battle. They are fearless and have posted no guards or the usual watchmen. That's why we are going to overrun them. They are buried deep in sleep, so it will be easy. Follow me as your leader, and I will give you this, my gray head, if things do not go as I say."[299]

Altar to Victory

The next morning . . . they put an eagle (battle standard) against the east door and they built an altar to victory following their ancestral error; they worshipped the one they call 'Mars' with their traditional rites. They worship an image of columns portraying Hercules, and the Sun, which the Greeks call Apollo. This shows how much they esteem these Gods, however misplaced this esteem may be. The Saxons think that they are descended from the Greeks because Hirmin or Hermis is called Mars in Greek. Nitwits still use this word even today for praising or blaming. For three days they celebrated their victory. They divided and hauled off the spoils of their enemies. They celebrated the funeral for the slain, praising their leader as they raised him to the sky. They hailed his celestial virtue, and divine spirit, and the steadiness that had driven them to achieve victory.[300]

Selecting War Leaders by Lot

If . . . a great war breaks out, a lot is drawn by which they select a leader whom all are expected to obey in prosecuting the war.[301]

A Religious Debate and Hot Iron

The Danes were Christians in the good old days, but they still worshipped idols with a gentile rite. The king was attending a certain feast when an argument arose over worshipping the gods. The Danes held that Christ was indeed a god, but that the other gods were greater since they gave more powerful omens and wonders to mortals. But a certain cleric, a bishop named Poppa, who is now leading a truly religious life, rose

---

[299] I, 11(rec. Kehr 16)
[300] ib. 12 (1. 1. 17s)
[301] ib. 14 (1. 1. 20)

against them, asserting that the one true god is the father with his only begotten son, our lord Jesus Christ, and the holy spirit. He also argued that the idols were really demons. He said he could prove that they were not Gods. King Harold, who was as slow to speak as he was quick to listen, then asked the cleric if he himself wanted to prove his faith. The bishop immediately agreed. The king ordered that the cleric be watched until the next day. In the morning, the king ordered a fire lit to heat a heavy chunk of iron and ordered the cleric to carry the white-hot iron to prove his faith.[302]

THIETMAR, BISHOP OF MERSEBERG

Thietmar, a Saxon, the second Bishop of Merseberg, lived from around 975 to around 1018. In 1004 he became bishop, and in 1009 he began a history of Merseberg which dilated into a history of the Holy Roman Empire and the Saxon Kings of Germany from 908 to 1018. He had gone to war against the Slavs with the Saxon King Henry II to recover Saxon lands, so part of the history is based on his own experience. He based this Chronicle *on earlier German Annals. His* Chronicle *contains other bits of folk custom not included here.*

CHRONICLE

The Sacred Spring Glozumi

Glozumi is a spring. It is not more than two miles from Albus and it generates a swamp. According to the locals and the testimony of numerous eyewitnesses, a marvel often occurs there. When a good peace is prophesied to the native population, and their land will not lie fallow, it is crammed with wheat, oats and nuts and its rich outpourings to them gladdens the hearts of the neighborhood. But when the savage storms of war are going to break out, it warns them by leaving signs of the future by leaving blood and ashes. However dubious their apprehension may be, they all venerate and fear this spring more than the church.[303]

Sacrifice in January

There is a place [the village of Selon] in these parts, which is the capitol of King Lederus. They all gather there every nine years in the month of January after we have celebrated the theophany of the Lord. There they sacrifice to their gods at least 99 men and as many horses and with dogs and roosters. As I said before, they think that with the commission of this crime they are serving and placating the gods when the offering is accepted.[304]

---

[302] III, 65 (1. 1. 117)

[303] Clemens p. 68: I, 3 (rec. Kurze 3)
[304] ib. 17 (1. 1. 11)

79

BURCHARD OF WORMS, CORRECTOR AND SOUL DOCTOR

Burchard was a cleric who became bishop of Worms in 1000. He died around 1025. He wrote the <u>Decretum</u>, *which contains the penitential material below in Book XIX. The Decretum contains many of the same decrees as those of the German Corrector above, and these overlapping passages have been left out.*

DECRETUM

Oaths by God's Head or Hair
If you have sworn by God's hair or head, or uttered other blasphemies against God, and you did it unconsciously, then pay with seven days on bread and water. ... If you swear by the heaven, earth or by the sun or the moon, or some other creature, you shall do penance for fifteen days on bread and water.[305]

Consulting Magicians
If you have brought sorcerers into your house for advice to learn a magical trick, or to avert one, or if you brought diviners in accordance with pagan tradition and ask them about the future as if they were prophets, or likewise from lot casters, or if you think lots will foretell the future, or if you consult augurers or those using incantations, you shall do penance for two years on the designated fast days.[306]

Ancestral Traditions
Have you practiced pagan traditions, which they treat as a hereditary right, and fathers always pass on to their sons with the devil's help, even to this very day? Such includes the worship of the elements, the moon, the sun, or the stars' courses. Do you try to bring back the glory of the new moon, or a lunar eclipse, by hollering? So you think these elements can help you, or that you could have power with them? Have you celebrated a marriage or built a new house on the new moon? [307]

Knots in Trees and on Crossroads
Have you made knots (*ligaturas*) or recited incantations, or those evil enchantments (*carmina*) used by bad men, swineherds, ploughmen, and sometimes hunters, as they recite devilish songs over bread or grass, or over certain vile knots? They hide these knots in a tree or cast them down at an intersection, or into a crossroads of two or three roads in order to relieve their animals or dogs from disease or destruction or to ruin others.[308]

Weaving
If you have participated in, or allowed the deceptions that women weave into the webs of their woolen work. When they start their webs they use incantations and by mingling

---

[305] Book XIX (Migne P.L. CXL) 35
[306] 60.
[307] 61.
[308] 63.

the warp and the woof, the incantations and the cloth become so intermingled that unless they add to these another incantation, they will all die.[309]

Herbs
Have you gathered herbs with evil incantations instead of using the Lord's prayer, the 'credo in Deum' and the 'paternoster'?[310]

Lighting Torches at Rocks and Springs, etc.
Have you gone to any place to pray other than a church or any religious place not authorized to you by your bishop or priest? Have you gone to springs, stones, trees, or crossroads, and set there a lit candle or torch? Have you taken bread to these places or other offerings, or have you eaten there, or sought healing of your body or mind?[311]

Bibliomancy
Have you tried to get auguries from codices or tablets, as many do customarily who think they can divine from psaltars, gospels, or other such things?[312]

Storm bringers
Have you believed or been involved in this unbelievable thing? Do you think that enchanters and those saying they are storm bringers, can cause storms or alter the minds of men?[313]

Mind Control
Have you believed in or been involved in this unbelievable thing in which women cast spells or recite incantations to change men's minds by turning hatred to love, love to hatred, or robbing their goods.?[314]

Diana's Wild Ride
Have you believed this unfaithful thing that evil women converted back to Satan, seduced by illusions, and the ghosts of demons believe and affirm? They think that the pagan goddess Diana and an unknown number of women ride on certain beasts and wander many parts of the world in the stillness of the night. They obey her orders as if she were their mistress and called to her service on certain nights. If only these people would just die in their perfidy and not bring others into the ruin of their aberration.[315]

Wakes
Have you observed any wakes? Have you attended a vigil over dead bodies in which the bodies of Christians are warded in a pagan ritual? Have you sung Satanic songs there

---

[309] 64.

[310] 65.

[311] 66.

[312] 67.

[313] 68.

[314] 69.

[315] 90. (This passage is followed by tirade on how astral projections are nothing more than the same dreams had by everyone.)

or danced any dances that pagans created through the teachings of Satan? Did you drink, relax, and laugh there? Did you leave off your compassion and charitable feelings? Have you behaved as if rejoicing over a brother's death?[316]

Satanic Letters

Have you made evil phylacteries using grass or amber, or the satanic letters which the devil drives some to make? Have you observed Thursday in honor of Jupiter?[317]

Playing Practical Jokes on Your Bishop

Have you plotted with other conspirators to make a mockery of your bishop by making a joke of his teachings or those of a priest?

Crossroads, Springs, Stones etc.

Have you eaten any sacrificial food given to idols? This includes offerings made at tombs, at springs, trees, stones, or crossroads. Have you carried stones to a heap of stones, or taken knots to the crosses set up at the crossroads? [318]

Costume Parties on January the First

Have you gone about in the guise of a stag or calf on January the first as the pagans do?[319]

New Years Projects

Have you done what some folks do on January the first? Have you wound 'Filare' on that holy night and spun or sewn? Have you begun whatever projects you were able because of the new year?[320]

Burning Churches

Have you burned down any churches or condoned this?[321]

Gossiping in Church

Some go to church and lip-sync the prayers for appearances to those around them while actually gossiping instead. They keep right on gossiping, even after the priest tells them to pray.[322]

---

[316] 91.

[317] 92.

[318] 94. On worship at crosses set up at crossroads for the expiation of murder in the later middle ages, see Mogk, Berichte und Verhandlungen der Sachsichen etc. Philol. Hist. Cl., LXXXI, (1929) 1-28

[319] 98. The Diocesian Council of Auxerre, held sometime between 561 and 605, decreed that "Disguising yourself as a stag or calf on the first of January is forbidden. An you cannot give Satanic gifts then either." See C. De Clercq. pp. 265-70. This council also mentions "lots of the saints" and forbids worship in private residences or villas. It also forbids the use of honey in eucharist wine. Whether these customs reflect the traditions of the German or the Romans is yet to be determined.

[320] 104.

[321] 136.

[322] 145.

Drinking Anti-Judgment Day Juice
Have you drunken holy oil to void God's judgment? Have you sought advice from others with anything made of grass, or wood, or stone or anything else that you have idiotically believed in? Have you held them in your mouth or had them sewn into your clothes, or tied to them yourself? Have you done any magic to overturn divine judgment?[323]

Footprints
Have you done what some satanic women sometimes do? They seek out christian footprints and paths. They dig up the footprints and watch them, hoping to ruin health.[324]

Burying Dead Children
Have you buried a dead child who was just born and baptized placing a wax paten in his left hand and a wax chalice filled with wine in his right, as some women do?[325]

Causing Impotence
Have you done as some adulteresses? When they find out that their lovers are going to get married, they snuff out their sexual desires and render them impotent by some magic trick such that they cannot consummate their marriages.[326]

Naked Honey and Grain Magic, Widdershins
Have you done what some women do? They pull off their clothes and spread honey all over their naked bodies. They lay their naked honey covered bodies upon wheat on a linen sheet spread across the ground. They start rolling back and forth, quite a bit, and then take off each grain of wheat clinging to their wet bodies. Then they put the wheat in a mill. They turn the mill backwards against the sun and grind it into flour. They make the flour into bread and feed it to their husbands so that they will weaken and waste away.[327]

Rainmaking
Have you done what some women do? When they need rain, they gather several girls and select one young maiden as their leader. They strip her and bring her naked away from the village to find some henbane, which is called 'Belissa' in German. They have the naked maiden dig out the herb with the pinky finger of her right hand. After digging it up they have her tie it to the little toe of her right foot with a string. Then they bring the maiden with the plant dragging behind her to the river. They are holding twigs and when they reach the river they sprinkle her with water using these twigs. They hope this magic will make rain. Then they bring her back from the river between their hands walking backwards like a crab.[328]

---

[323] 167.
[324] 175.
[325] c. 185.
[326] c. 186.
[327] c. 193.
[328] 194.

RIMBERT ABBOT OF LEUCONAY

Rimbert, the Abbot of Leucony, wrote this biography of Walaric in the middle of the 11th century. Walaric was a hermit who lived from the mid 6th century to 619. He founded a hermitage in Leuconay with a grant of land from the Nuestrian king, Clotaire. The hermitage eventually became a monastery.

THE LIFE OF WALARIC, ABBOT OF LEUCONAY

A Great Statue

By the bank of the river Auvae, there was a great offering embellished with all kinds of images. It had been donated and sent there into the land for its high quality. The country folk worshipped it in a big way in accordance with their national religious rites. When the confessor saw this, he suddenly burned with zeal for God and he said to the boy: "My son, throw it down into its destruction." The boy never hesitated, he followed the order. He merely touched it with his hand. The immense weight, which could be moved only by the great multitude of men and could hardly be cut by axes, suddenly made a thunderous noise and with a great rush fell to the ground as if it were wet and rotten. The whole thing appeared to be smashed to pieces; and all at the touch of one obedient monk.

But from all directions they came for a fight with arms and clubs. They shamefully attacked one after another as if they would avenge the injury to their god. When they suddenly attacked the clerics all at once with a great fury, their blows and strokes were suspended in the air with their arms stretched out. The confessor, who was always intrepid and robust of spirit, said this to them: "If the lord permits them to continue, no one will be able to stop them."[329]

BERTINI

The monk Bertini wrote this biography of King Cnut in the mid 11th century. Cnut was a son of The Danish King Swein Forkbeard who lived from the late 10th century to around 1035. He helped his father invade England. He became the leader when his father died. In 1017 he became king of England.

THE DEEDS OF KING KNUT

The Raven Banner

The Danes had a marvelous battle standard. The reader may be incredulous, but I say that it is true and that my sources are accurate. The standard was woven with the most pure and white silk. There was no image on it. But during wartime a raven would appear on it as if it were embroidered onto the silk. In their victories the raven's wings would appear to be flapping, its beak open and its feet moving vigorously. But in defeat, its whole body would be still and drooping. Thorkil, the leader in the first battle, sought an

---

[329] 22 (M.G. Scr. rer. Mer. IV, 168 s.):

omen from the standard and said: "Let us fight valiantly, comrades. We do not face any danger today. This is proven by the moving raven on our foreknowing standard."[330]

WOLFHER

Wolfher wrote this biography around 1045. Godard was born in 960 and lived to 1038. Godard became a monk in 991 at the Abbey of Altaich and became a bishop in Hildesheim in 1021.

THE LIFE OF BISHOP GODEHARD

A Sacred Spring
In the eastern part of our city of Hildisheim . . . there was a terrifying swamp. All who lived around it hated and feared it because, as it was believed, they either heard or saw certain terrible illusions, and as much during the midday as at night. Since it came from a brackish spring that bubbled up in the middle of the swamp, it was called "Salty."[331]

ADAM OF BREMEN

The German historian and geographer Adam of Bremen wrote The Deeds of the Bishops of the Church of Hamburg between 1074 and 1076. In 1069 he began running the cathedral school in Bremen. In his works he describes Iceland, Greenland, Scandinavia, and even mentions Vinland.

THE DEEDS OF THE BISHOPS OF THE CHURCH OF HAMBURG

Heruli
The neighbors of the Suevi were those known as Druids, Bardi, Sicambri, Huns, Vandals, Sarmatians, Lombards, Heruli, Dacians, Marcomanni, Goths, and Slavs.[332]

Natural Law
If any Saxons marry outside their rank, they are given the death penalty. The Saxons also enforce good laws for the punishment of bad deeds. To promote good ethical conduct, they have striven to have many honorable laws that accord with natural law. These would be very helpful to them in earning true happiness if they were not ignorant of their creator and ignorant of the truth of his worship.[333]

---

[330] II, 9 (M.G. Scr.. XIX, 517)
[331] 20 (M.G. Scr. XI, 207)
[332] I, 3
[333] ib. I, 6

Irminsul

The Saxons also worshipped a large tree trunk erected in the open. In Saxon it was called *Irminsul*, which in Latin means "Universal Column" as if it sustained everything.[334]

Convert or Die

When Charlemagne conquered and subjugated all who resisted, he proposed this condition on the Saxons; they must quit devil worship and their traditional rites . . . and join the Franks and become a single nation.[335]

Bashing Frisian Idols

The Angle Willihad burned with the desire to get martyred, so he went to Frisia. He loitered at the blessed martyr Boniface's tomb and baptized thousands of the faithful and those who repented of the martyrdom. He is said to have gone about idol bashing and converting people to the true god.[336]

Thing at Birka

King Olaf was at the people's Thing at Birka. . . . Ansgar found that the king had gained a favorable response from the lots and from an idol. The people agreed and the king ordered that Ansgar be allowed to build a church there and granted everyone permission to get baptized.[337]

A Religious Counterrevolutionary

Horic ascended the Danish throne. He drove out God's priests and shut down the churches because of his innate and ferocious anger against the Christians.[338]

Weapon Oaths

The two sides' negotiators had been sent to the river Eider. They swore on their weapons to a solid peace, in accordance with their ancestral traditions.[339]

Uppsala

Birka is a Gothic town in Sweden. It is not far from the temple called Uppsala, which the Swedes think the greatest for the worship of their gods.[340]

Not Easily Convinced

The North men had totally forgotten about Christianity and were not easily convinced.[341]

---

[334] ib. 1, 7.
[335] ib. 1, 10
[336] ib. 1, 12
[337] ib. 1, 28
[338] ib. 1, 30
[339] ib. 1, 39
[340] I, 60 (62, ed. Schmeidler 58):
[341] 1. 63:

Swedes Go Back to their Old Ways
The Swedes and the Goths, who were first introduced to Christianity by Ansgar, went back to paganism.[342]

Giant Descent and Ivar
Haakan was cruel. He was descended from Ivar (the Boneless) and giants.[343]

Forced Converts
Then the Danish king Svein Otto, Harold's son, got involved in plots against his father and sought advice from folks his father had forced to convert to Christianity.[344]

Magicians
According to some, Olaf was Christian, others say he lapsed from the faith, but they all say he was a talented diviner and lot caster and that he had the utmost faith in auguries by birds. They nicknamed him "Legbone" (Krakkaben) because of it. They also say that he was a magician and that he maintained these magicians who were overrunning the land in his own household as his associates. They deluded him with their error and he died.[345]

Swamp Worshippers
Unwan completely eliminated all the pagan rites that the swamp worshippers frequent with idiotic reverence. It was as if they had been banished from the light. Their religion still throve in that land. He had new churches built throughout the diocese in the stead of those holy groves our lowland folk had so often worshipped.[346]

Demons
They said that one of Olaf's good qualities, among others, was a great zeal for God. He ruined the witches of the region as their numbers had gushed forth along with their barbarities. These monstrosities were especially plentiful in Norway. Diviners, augerers, magicians, enchanters, and other satellites of the antichrist lived there. Demons toyed with their trapped and unhappy minds using illusions and wonders.[347]

Uppsala and Oppression
The Swedish Olaf had a similar zeal. He wanted to convert these subdued peoples to Christianity, so he strove to ruin the temple and idols at Uppsala in central Sweden. The pagans feared his desires and agreed with the king that if he wanted to be Christian, he could have his favorite part of Sweden in which to establish the church and Christianity, but he could not force any people to give up worshipping their own gods, but would have to let them convert to Christ of their own free will.[348]

---

[342] 1. 63
[343] ib. II, 22
[344] ib. II, 25
[345] II, 38:
[346] ib. II, 48 (46, 1. 1. 108)
[347] ib. 57 (55 1. 1. 117)
[348] ib. II, 58 (56 1. 1. 118)

Then they stirred up a rebellion against the foremost and most blessed King Olaf. Olaf accused their women of practicing witchcraft and drove them from the kingdom of Norway. . . . Olaf believed that he had been restored to the Norwegian throne for so bravely acting against his enemies and for justly opposing their rites. Therefore he spared none who wanted to remain a magician or refused to convert to Christianity. He almost completely fulfilled his oaths when a few surviving magicians cut him down for all those he had executed.[349]

Thor Statue
An Angle named Wolfred became smitten with a holy love. He went to Sweden and very bravely preached God's word and thereby turned many to Christianity. A popular idol called Thor stood in the pagan *Thing* (law assembly). Wolfred railed against it and then got his double bitted axe and smashed the idol to smithereens. This audacity got him stabbed a thousand times. . . . The barbarians mutilated and derided his corpse and sunk it in a swamp.[350]

Hanging Upside Down Between Two Dogs
Theitmar's son caught Arnold himself a few days later and hanged him by the legs between two dogs.[351]

Amazons
God's anger followed the Danes for driving out their bishop. The kings sent one of his sons named Anund to conquer new land. Anund went into a land of women; we think they were Amazons. The women poisoned the springs so that Anund and his host died there.[352]

Christians Versus Magicians
Harold destroyed numerous churches . . . Harold was a slave to the sorcery and the worthless man did not care that his holy brother had eradicated such monstrosities from the kingdom and that he struggled up to his death to embrace the tenets of Christianity.[353]

Bishop Gets Heathen Religion
The bishop abandoned the truth for fables and dreams. . . They say he started getting into magic.[354]

Seeress
In those days a woman who had the pythian spirit came and publicly announced that the archbishop would die within two years if he did not convert.[355]

---

[349] ib. (59 1. 1. 120 s.)
[350] ib. II, 59
[351] ib. III, 8
[352] ib. III, 15
[353] ib. III, 17 (16, 1. 1. 159)
[354] ib III 61
[355] ib. III 64 (63, 1. 1. 210)

Frigg Statue
They also say that he busted apart a much-honored statue of Frigg.[356]

Amazons and Dog-Headed Apes
They say that the Amazons live along the Baltic shore in what is known as the 'Land of Women.' Some say that the Amazons sip water to get pregnant. Others say that visiting merchants or their captive males impregnate them. Still others say they conceive by the various monsters that are common in that land. We think this theory is more believable. If these women bear male children, they grow up into dog-headed apes (*cynocephali*). The females grow up to be lovely ladies. They live alone and forcefully turn away the men who come around. The dog-headed apes have their heads on their chests. They speak by barking and are often seen as captives in Russia. . . .

War Dogs
Dogs guard their nation. The Alans array their dogs in a military formation when they have to do battle.[357]

Hospitality
The Swedes think it a terrible disgrace to deny travelers hospitality. They give all hospitalities to a traveler for as many days as he wants to stay. They compete with each other to take the traveler to the houses of their friends. These are the good points in their tradition.

They are also very hospitable to the truth preachers who are wise and chaste. They even let bishops attend the common folk assembly known as the "*warh*."[358]

Lots
When they transact private business, they consult lots, but in public matters they traditionally seek answers from demons, as The Life of Ansgar tells us.[359]

Christ the War God
In grave combat situations they call on one of their many gods for help. If they win, they worship and exalt that one above all the others. They now commonly agree that the christian God is the most powerful of all.[360]

More Amazons and Dog-Headed Apes
Hordes of humanoid monstrosities prevent access to that which lies beyond. Amazons live there, along with dog-headed apes, cyclopes with eyes on their foreheads, and what Solinus calls Himantapodes, which are flesh-loving cannibals who hop around on one foot. [361]

---

[356] ib. IV, 8 (1. 1. 210)
[357] ib. IV 19
[358] ib. IV 21
[359] Schol. 133 (128, 1. 1. 252 s)
[360] ib. IV 22
[361] ib. IV 25

Temple at Uppsala

Their most notable temple is close to Birka and Sigtuna and is known as Uppsala. This temple is ornamented all in gold and houses three idols of gods they worship. Thor is enthroned in the center of the room. Wodan and Frikko are placed on each side. Here is what these gods are about: They say Thor rules the air which controls thunder and lightening, winds, clouds, good weather and harvests. Wodan, that is furor, is a war God who gives men courage against their foes. The third is Frikko who gives people peace and sensual pleasure. They endow his statue with a huge phallus. They depict Woden as armed, as our folk traditionally depicted Mars. Thor is shown with a scepter, like Jove. They worship men they have made into Gods. They attributed immortality and great deeds to them, just as they did to King Eric in the Life of Ansgar.[362]

Divine Functions

They designate special priests for making offerings to each God on their behalf. When disease and famine threaten, they give offerings to a statue of Thor. In war, they give offerings to Wodan. For Weddings, they make offerings to Frikko. The entire population of all the provinces of Sweden customarily gathers at a great religious feast every nine years. Every one has to go to this solemn celebration. Kings and people all send gifts to Uppsala.

What is crueler than any penalty is that Christians redeem themselves at these ceremonies. They traditionally appease their Gods with the blood of the sacrifice of nine heads of each kind of male animal. They hang the bodies in a holy grove near the temple. They think that this is such a sacred grove that every single tree has become divine by the death and sacrificial rot. They even hang dogs and horses along with men. A seventy two year old Christian told me that the hanging corpses were intermingled. Not only that, but the songs they traditionally sing at this kind of rite of libation are so disgraceful and so many that I would rather not even talk about them. [363]

Uppsala's Great Tree

A gigantic tree stands near this temple extending its branches broadly. It is green in summer and winter alike. No one knows what kind it is. The pagans also have a sacrificial spring into which they plunge human victims. If they cannot recover the body, they think their prayers have been answered.[364]

Arctic Magicians

Those who live beyond the arctic along the sea are thought pre-eminent in magic and spells. They pull up huge whales out of the ocean and onto the shore with booming incantations. They do many other magical things that have been described in the scriptures . . . Aurochs, buffaloes and elk are hunted there as in Sweden. . . . They were all given over to witchcraft at first . . .[365]

---

[362] ib. 26
[363] ib. VI 27
[364] Schol. 139 (135, 1. 1. 257 s.)
[365] ib. VI (1. 1. 265 s.)

Temple Chains at Uppsala

A golden chain surrounds the temple and hangs from its gables. You can see its red glow as you draw near. The shrine itself is on level ground but it is like a theater because of the surrounding hills.[366]

Nine Day Feast

They feast and sacrifice like that for nine days. They sacrifice one human each day, along with one of each of the other creatures. They sacrifice seventy-two creatures in nine days. They make this sacrifice at the vernal equinox.[367]

On Heathen Burials

They do not believe in the resurrection of the body, but they still hold very reverential funeral rites in accordance with ancient Roman customs. They bury the dead with money, arms and other possessions dear to the departed while alive. This has been said of the Indians as well. Such things are commonly found in their graves because it is one of their ancient folk traditions to order treasure buried in amphorae or other vessels.[368]

CHRONICON OF SAINT NEOTI

This compilation of sources for English history was made no later than the beginning of the 12th Century. The compiler is unknown. The manuscripts was discovered in the priory of St. Neots and contains excerpts from another biography of St. Neots. Most of this compilation is drawn from the Anglo-Saxon Chronicle, Bede's History of the English Church, the works of King Alfred, and Abbo of Fluery's Life of St. Edmund.

The Raven Banner

There the Christians took a great deal of plunder, including the raven banner. It is said that the three sisters of Ingwar and Hubba, the daughters of Lodbrok, wove that standard and finished the job between the dawn and dusk of a single day. If is further said that every time the standard was at a battle's forefront it would tell whether its bearers would win or not. If not, the raven on the center of the banner would appear living and flying if they were going to win. If its bearers were to be vanquished, it would be still and appear downcast. This has been proven many times.[369]

MIRACLES OF SAINT MATHIUS

Written in the 12th Century by an unknown author concerning miracles of the Apostle Mathew. Some of his relics had been transferred to Trier where they worked many miracles.

---

[366] Schol. 139 (135, 1. 1. 258)
[367] Schol. 141 (137, 1. 1. 260)
[368] Schol. 144 (140, 1. 1. 264)
[369] ad. a 878 (ed. W.H. Stevenson, Asser's Life of the King Alfred,)

91

Neptune

A small boy fell out of a boat by a bridge on the Moselle. A young man saw this. Throwing off his clothes, he jumped into the river to rescue to rescue the boy. But an evil spirit named Neptune pulled him under and drowned him.[370]

WILLIAM OF MALMESBURY

The English historian William of Malmesbury lived from around 1090 to 1143. He worked as a librarian at Malmesbury's Abbey. Bede was one his models for historical writing and he wrote a church history as well as <u>Deeds of the English Kings</u>, which he wrote between around 1125 and 1127. <u>Deeds</u> covers the period from 449 to 1127.

DEEDS OF THE ENGLISH KINGS

Hengist and Horsa

The war band came to Britain from Germany. It was a small band, but it made up for its size with bravery. Their two leaders were Hengist and Horsa. They were not of obscure ancestry in their own country, and they had high character. They were the great grandsons of the most ancient Woden, from whom almost all the barbarian royal families think they are sprung and to whom the deluded Saxons have consecrated every fourth day of the week. To his wife Frea they consecrated every sixth day. This is still practiced today.[371]

DEEDS OF THE ABBOTS OF TRUDON

An unknown monk of the Abbey of Trudon wrote this between 1136 and 1138.

Sacred Ship on Wheels Dragged from Town to Town

There was a kind of laborer whose job was to weave yarn from flax and wool. They were commonly thought brash and overbearing over the other laborers. To avenge an injury to himself and to dash their pride and brashness, a pauper from the town of Inda devised this diabolical trick. Judges accepted a pledge and frivolous men who love jokes and novelties helped him to build a boat in a nearby forest.[372]

They mounted the boat on wheels so that it could roll across the land. He got the nobles to let him have the weavers drag the boat with ropes over their shoulders from Inda to Aquisgrani. From there, a grand parade of male and female weavers dragged the boat to Traiectum where they put an emblem on its evil sail. From there they took it to Tungris and then to Los.

Abbot Rudolph then heard about the coming ship and the evil portent with which it was imbued. It came with inauspicious portent and a zeal for heathenism. The abbot had a prescient mind and warned his people not to receive the ship. He warned that the

---

[370] (M.G., SCR VIII, 232)
[371] 5 (ed. Stubbs, I, 9)
[372]

bringers' hearts were filled with malice and were doing it as a trick. He told them that the force of sedition drove the ship and it would bring fire, slaughter, pillage, and the shedding of lots of blood. But they did not want to listen.

The town of Los delayed that image of evil spirits that Rudolph had condemned for all of those days. They gladly welcomed this fatal Trojan horse and brought it into the town square and consecrated it, where they were about to die for it. Immediately the village weavers received a judgment of proscription and they slowly came to be the profane sentries of that idol.

Pope! Who of all of mankind has ever seen such a thing, if I can say it in Latin, such brutality by rational animals since Christ was reborn? A sentence of proscription compelled the weavers to cram the ship full of all kinds of arms and to keep a continuous and anxious watch over it during the day and night. It was a miracle they did not force them to sacrifice enemies to Neptune before the ship, as was customary in that region. But Neptune reserved them for Mars to whom he wanted to grant human sacrifices.

The weavers invoked the just God with a hidden heartfelt groan, praying for deliverance from, and help against, those casting them into such degradation. After all, they had led honorable lives similar to those of the early Christians and apostles who had also been manual laborers. They worked day and night to feed and clothe themselves and to provide for their children. They gathered and griped and cried about how the abuses were directed against themselves and not against other merchants: especially since they were living such good lives in an age when Christians were indulging in so many bad activities. They declared that the only ignoble things were those that brought impurity and transgression into the heart. They also said that it was better to be poor rustic weavers than orphan taxers, widow robbers, or aristocratic judges.

As they griped about these and other things, a great racket erupted from that house of malignant spirits. The noise came from various kinds of disgraceful songs that were unworthy of Christian choruses. I do not know if this sound came from Bacchus, Venus, Neptune, Mars, or from whom.

The judges pronounced the ship sacred, but before any of the weavers approached to touch it, they announced that unless the weavers redeemed themselves with a libation, that their pledges would be taken from the hill. But what can I say? Should I speak or be silent? How I wish lies were falling from my lips.

Under their God's dim light, the moonlight that is, their women shucked off their female decency at the sound of the frivolous tumult. They sprang from their beds, some half naked, and others clad only in cloaks. They wantonly sang along with the leader and romped around the ship. When this cursed dance broke out, a loud and confused vocal clamor erupted as both sexes began bachanizing (copulating in a very celebratory way) with each other.

They celebrated these terrible rites for more than twelve days.[373]

HERWARD'S DEEDS

HERWARD'S DEEDS was written in the mid 12th century by an unknown author. Herward was an English resistance leader in post-conquest Norman England.

Witches and a Spring
That night Herward heard the widow and the witch speaking in Latin. They talked of how they should quit working and conquer the island. They thought that Herward was just a farmer and could not understand them. Herward saw them leave in the midnight calm to a garden. The garden was by a house a little ways away. In the garden spring waters rose and flowed to the east. Herward followed them and listened to them at a distance. I do not know who the spring's guardian was, but they were waiting for responses to their questions.[374]

GEOFFREY OF MONMOUTH

Geoffrey was a teacher and writer in Oxford in the 1130s and he finished his History of the Kings of Britain in the latter part of that decade. Geoffrey wrote the History to glorify the Anglo-Norman past and the work took the form of a kind of historical romance.

HISTORY OF THE KINGS OF BRITAIN

The Wassail Story: Hengist, Renwein and Vortigern
Hengist, the Saxon's spokesman, answered Vortigern: "Noblest of all kings, we are from Saxony, a part of Germany. We come looking for work, from yourself or another king. We had to leave Saxony and here's why. Saxony has a custom that required our departure. Whenever the country becomes overpopulated, the provincial leaders call forth all the kingdom's young males to gather before them. They cast lots to determine who among them is most strong and able. The chosen are required to travel into foreign countries to earn a living. . . . Our leaders cast lots. The lots picked the lads you see before you now. The leaders ordered them to obey the custom. My brother and I were elected to lead them because we are of the royal family. I am Hengist and my brother is Horsa. We embarked with only Mercury to guide us, and arrived at your kingdom."

At the mention of the name "Mercury," the king looked straight at them and asked them what their religion was. Hengist answered: "We worship our nation's gods, including Saturn, Jove and the others who have dominion over this world. We especially worship Mercury, who is called Woden in Saxon. Our forebears named the fourth day of the

---

[373] XII, 11 s. (MG Scr. X 309 s.)

[374] (Hardy and Martin, L'estoria des Engles solum la Translatcion Maistre Geffrei Gaimer, I, 385)

week after him and it is called Wednesday to this day. Next we worship Freia, who is the mightiest of all the Goddesses. We named the sixth day of the week after her and call it Friday."[375]

Meanwhile the messengers returned from Germany and brought back 17 ships full of crack troops. Even Hengist's daughter, Renwein, whose beauty was second to none, came along. After their arrival, Hengist invited King Vortigern into his hall so that he would see the new building and new warriors whom they had invited over. King Vortigern came in disguise and he praised the rapid construction and the soldiers that he had invited and retained.

As he was being refreshed at a royal feast, the young lady came from her chamber bearing a golden goblet filled with wine. She went up to the king and on bent knee said: "Lord King, Wassail (*waesseil*)!" The young lady's face and charm stunned the king, and made him quite excited. Finally, he asked his interpreter what the young lady said and how he should respond. The interpreter said: "She called you Lord King and honored you with a salutation in her language. You should respond by saying 'Drink Hail! (*drincheil*)'" Vortigern then responded by saying "Drink Hail!" He commanded the lady to drink and he then took the drink from her hand, kissed her, and drank himself. From that day on it has remained the custom in Britain that one who drinks to someone at a feast says "wassail!", and the one who drinks next responds: "Drink hail!" (*drincheil*).

But Vortigern was drunk on a different kind of intoxicant. He was in love with the young lady and demanded to see her father. Satan had entered his heart for he was a Christian and wanted to marry a pagan. . . . They did not dally. Vortigern got Renwein, and Hengist got the province of Kent. Voritgern married the pagan lady that same night. She gratified him beyond all measure.[376]

SAXO GRAMMATICUS

Saxo Grammaticus wrote this Danish history in the late twelfth century for the purpose of generating national pride. He hoped that his work would rank among the world's great nationalistic literary achievements, such as Virgil's Aeneid.

DEEDS OF THE DANES

Damned Souls Scream from the Ice
Great masses of ice flow to Iceland at certain fixed times. This ice smashes into the rough coast and its resounding echo may be heard from the crags. It sounds like the roar of many loud voices howling out strange shouts from the depths. This is why they think that the evil souls of the damned are paying for their evil lives and the magnitude of their offenses in icy tortures.[377]

---

[375] iv 10
[376] vi 11, ib. vi 12
[377] (ed. Holder 7)

Giants and Old Howe Hills

A race of giants once worked the soil of that part of Denmark, as shown by the big rocks affixed to old howe hills and caves. Anyone who does not believe that some monstrous force did this should go look at how tall these hills are and then explain how such gigantic rocks got on top of these hills. . . . We do not know whether post-flood giants or some really strong humans did this. Our people say that such monsters, with superhuman strength, live in the remote, rocky, uninhabitable, and inaccessible solitudes that we discussed earlier. Their bodies can change, giving them the amazing ability to appear and disappear. They can be in your presence one minute but then they are suddenly gone.[378]

Voting Rocks

The ancients used to elect their kings by standing on rocks firmly embedded into the ground to declare their votes. They thought that the solidity of the rocks would adumbrate the endurance of their deeds.[379]

Goat Hide and a Giantess

Bess found out that the Swedish king Sytrygg's daughter was engaged to marry a giant. He condemned the inappropriate joining of the royal line and started a war against the Swedes. He wanted to exercise Herculean courage against the might of giants. He put on goat hides to strike fear into everyone he met and crossed into Gotland. Bess was decked out in all those animal hides and wielding a fearful club with his right hand; he looked like a giant. He encountered Groa as he she was riding toward the forest pools for a bath.[380]

A Gift Seals a Pact

Accept this red gold from me and may this gift seal an enduring pact and a sturdy fidelity between us and may it make fast our marriage.[381]

Gold Nail

A soothsayer told him that he could only defeat Sigtrygg with gold. He fixed a gold nail into his wooden club.[382]

Mathematicians

There were three bizarre kinds of mathematicians that each worked its own brand of illusions. The first kind were huge beings who were far bigger than humans whom ancients called giants. The second kind had become the best in divination and was superb in the Delphic craft. The giants had bigger bodies, but the diviners had livelier intellects. The diviners and the giants were constantly engaging in great wars for dominance. The magicians had victory and crushed the giant race with arms. The magicians not only won the right to rule, but even passed a law saying they were gods.

---

[378] ib. (1. 1. 8 s.)
[379] 10.
[380] ib. I
[381] 17
[382] 17

Both kinds are good at tricking the eye and able to exchange shapes with others and able to disguise themselves with false appearances.

More Mathematicians
The first two types interbred and generated a third, but these were not as big or as smart. Their minds were tricked by the delusions of the others they thought gods.[383]

Symbols Carved in Wood
They came to the house during the sad funeral of the late household head. To divine the intentions of the gods, Harthgrepa carved symbols into a piece of wood while rhythmically singing fearful songs. She instructed Hadding to place the wood under the dead man's tongue. The dead man suddenly began speaking in a horrible sounding voice and sang this song:

An Underworld Soul
"I am an underworld soul. Let whoever invoked me be drawn down to the hellish deep, be damned, and die horribly."[384]

Harthgrepa grew to her giant shape by unfolding her limbs and grabbed the hand so that Hadding could chop it off. More pus than blood poured out of the wounded hand.[385]

One-Eyed Man and a Blood Pact
A one-eyed old man felt sorry for the lonely Hadding. . . . He brought Hadding into companionship with the viking, Liser, and had them make a pact. Our ancestors used to seal pacts by sprinkling and mingling together their blood in their footprints.

They went to war against Loker, the Kurlandish king, but they were beaten. . . . the old man brought Hadding to his hall on his own steed. . . . He gave him prophetic advice by singing as follows.

Fetters
"Your enemy will think you are running away when you go, and will strike and chain you in fetters. Thus will he give you to a wild beast's teeth to be torn and eaten. You need to ply your guard's ears with numerous stories. When he has finished eating, he will sleep soundly. Then break the binding chains. Come back a little later when you have risen up and attack the beast with all your might. This beast eagerly flings its prey about. Try your main against its fore-flanks and test your naked sword against its heart sinews. Then bring your throat to its pouring blood and let your hungry jaws feast upon its corpse. New might will invigorate your body and unexpected energy will fill your muscles and your sinews will draw up and gather strength.[386]

---

[383] 19
[384] And so the curse goes on in this vein for several more lines. ed.
[385] 22 (1.1. 22)
386 386

Odin

At that time in Europe, a certain Odin was wrongly thought to be a god. He usually stayed in Uppsala more than in other places either because of its charm or its people's laziness. Odin's habits thereby dignified Uppsala. The northern kings wanted to attend to his name with a more weighty religious practice. They built a golden idol in his likeness. They covered the statue's arms with weighty armbands. With the highest pretense of religious of sentiment, they sent the statue to Byzantium as a proof of their respect. His popularity made him so happy that he eagerly kissed the sender's precious gift.

Frigg

Frigg, his wife, summoned craftsmen to take gold from the statue so that she could go about in better style than Odin. Odin hanged them and had his statue set on a pedestal. By an amazing feat of engineering, it would speak when touched by a human. Nevertheless, Frigg put the glamour of her own cult before her spouse's divine glory. She subjected herself to sex with a servant, whose genius destroyed the statue. Frigg used the gold that had been given to public worship as a personal luxury. This woman was unworthy of marriage to a god; she thought nothing of pursuing shamelessness if she could more readily satiate her greed.

Both of Frigg's insults wounded Odin deeply. He was pained by the damage to his statue as much as by Frigg's infidelity. These twin disgraces wounded him so deeply that he went into exile filled with a genuine sense of dishonor. He thought that his exile would abolish dishonor's sordid sting.

Mithothyn

A certain Mithothin was famous for his success with magic tricks. It was as if he was invigorated by a heavenly gift when Odin left, for Mithothyn exploited the occasion to pretend godhead himself. He enveloped the minds of the barbarians with shadowy and novel errors. His fame as a magician led them to perform ceremonies in his name. He also opposed the notion that divine anger or profanation of the holy could be handled with confused and mixed sacrifices. He prohibited the invocation of vows in common and arranged for separate sacrifices for each god.

Odin came back. Mithothyn abandoned magic, and went into hiding in Phoenicia where a mob of locals killed him. His evil endured even after he died. Sudden death took those who approached his grave mound. After he died, so many bad diseases emerged from him, that he seemed to have left behind more terrible monuments to himself than in life. It was as though he was wreaking vengeance on his killers. Because of this horror, the locals dug up his grave and drove a sharp stake through his heart and cut off his head. That's how the folk remedied that problem.

Then Odin's wife died and Odin was able to rehabilitate the pristine clarity of his reputation and the stain on his divine status, so he came out of hiding. He then compelled all the folks who had usurped his divine honors in his absence to relinquish their divine titles as if they had never belonged to them.

The divine brilliance of his arrival broke up the bands of magicians as if they were shadows. Besides depriving them of divinity, he even made them leave the country. Those who so wrongly forced themselves upon heaven deserved to be forced from the land.[387]

Funerary Suicide
Asmund's wife, Gunnhild, did not want to outlive him so she robbed herself of her own spirit with steel. She preferred to follow her husband into the grave than to abandon him by living. Their friends entrusted her body to the grave, adding her remains to the ashes of her husband. They thought she was worthy of her husband's tomb since she preferred her beloved to life itself.[388]

A Voice
At bedtime, a voice of unknown origin sang this song to the camp and to the Danes who were pressed by extreme desperation.

> *You have abandoned your household gods and your county under a terrible portent?*
> *What vain ideas deceive your minds?*[389]

This prophecy was fulfilled in the morning when a throng of Danes was killed. The following night a similar voice of unknown origin fell upon the ears of the Danish youth.

> *Why does Uffi provoke me thus with grave sedition?*
> *He will pay the ultimate penalty.*
> *He will be attacked and stabbed by many spears.*[390]

Hadding Kills a Benign God
Hadding was beaten and sought refuge in Halsingland. There he escaped the sun's fervor by washing himself in the cold ocean water. He attacked an unknown kind of beast. He dealt out many blows and killed it. Then he drew the corpse into his camp. A woman met him as he was celebrating his victory and she told him this:

> "... *Your sacrilegious hands have slain a being from above who was enveloped in an alien body. You are the killer of a kind god. But when the sea has you, the Aeolian wind will unleash its fury from its prison. The Zephyr and Boreas will rush down on you. The Auster, the east wind, will run you down. They will cooperate and compete in blasting you with winds, until you soften the divine severity with prayer.* ...

---

[387] (1.1.25 s.)
[388] (1. 1. 27)
[389]

[390] ib. (1. c. 29 s.)

Froblot

When he got back, Hadding constantly suffered from all kinds of things; he thereby disturbed the peace everywhere he went. A vast and powerful cloud rose up as he was sailing and overwhelmed his fleet. His ship broke apart. When he sought out lodgings, these were suddenly destroyed as well. He could not get any relief from this evil until he expiated his crime with sacrifices and heaven's grace could return to him. In fact, he sacrificed bad enemies to the god Fro to regain divine favor. He performed this sacrifice repeatedly every year as a customary part of a time of holidays. The Swedes call this the Froblot.[391]

Woman Chooses a Husband by Feeling Men's Legs

Reginhild could not tell the identity of her rescuer because he was so wounded, but she assiduously nursed his wound-rent body back to health. She stuck a ring into a gash in one of his legs to mark him out so she could recognize him later. When her father granted her the liberty of deciding who her spouse would be, she inspected the lads gathered at the feast. She groped the limbs of each one carefully, in search of the hidden ring.[392]

Hadding Goes Down There

A lady by the stove bore in some hemlock. She was seen stretching her head from the floor toward Hadding as he was eating and offering him the folds of her garment. From what part of the world came these fresh herbs during the winter? She knew what the king wanted and she wrapped him in her own cloak and disappeared leading him down under the earth. I think that the underworld gods decided to bring him alive to the realm where he would go after death.

Hadding and the woman first pierced into a foggy gloom and walked a road carved by ages of walking. They saw leaders wearing togas and purple cloaks. They left these behind and came, at last, to a sunny place. There grew the herbs that the lady had brought.

River of Weapons

A bit further on, Hadding and the woman ran into a violently rushing river whose bluish black water twisted all kinds of weapons in its rapid eddies. They crossed over on a bridge and saw the clashing of two battle lines of similar warriors. Hadding asked the lady who they were. She told him that these were men slain by iron. Thus they testify to their manner of death in this endless performance. In this spectacle they are emulating the deeds of their previous lives.

The Rooster

As they continued, a wall blocked their way. It was hard to approach or cross this wall, but the lady tried jump it nevertheless. Her thin and wrinkled physique did not help her and she failed. Then she wrung a rooster's neck and hurled the rooster across the

---

[391] ib. (1. c. 29)
[392] (1. 1. 30)

defensive wall. The bird suddenly came back to life and its loud crowing proved that its breath had returned.[393]

Storm bringing

An old man on Hadding's side opposed and drove back the enemy's cloud mass with his own clouds. Upon leaving, the old man predicted that the victorious Hadding would not die at the hands of enemies, but would instead end his own life voluntarily.[394]

Hadding Likes the Ocean, His Wife Prefers the Woods

But rural life was dear to Hadding's wife who could not stand the singing of the sea birds in the morning. In the following verses she shows how she loved wandering in the woods.[395]

A Dream

After doing all that, Hadding went to sleep and saw an apparition of his dead wife as she sang to him thus:

> *a bairn of yours will soothe the untamed raging beast*
> *and its terrible jaws will rend angry wolves.*
> ... *Watch out! A bird born to you, an evil owl, and a swan with a singing voice, is*
> *dangerous to you.*

In the morning, when the king arose from his slumber, he described his vision to a wise conjecturer. He interpreted the wolf as Hadding's son, who would be ferocious in the future. He said the swan denoted his daughter. The first was going to smite his enemies, the other was going to plan intrigues against her father.[396]

Honoring a Dead Hero

In the meantime, the Swedish King, Hunding, had been told that Hadding was dead, which was bogus. Hunding summoned his nobles to pay homage to the dead Hadding and had a large earthenware vessel filled to capacity with ale. He directed that it be set in the center of the party. To make a special occasion of it, he did not neglect the crowd and took the part of a waiter with no reluctance. As he was going about the court discharging these services, he slipped and fell into the vat. He drowned and his spirit left him. Maybe Orcus was punishing him for trying to placate him with false acts of obsequy, or perhaps for falsely thinking Hadding was dead. When Hadding found out, he repaid Hunding's veneration with equal gratitude. He did not want to survive the departed Hunding, so he hung himself as the people looking on.[397]

---

[393] (1.1. 31)
[394] (1.1. 32)
[395] (1. 1. 32)
[396] (1.1. 35)
[397] (1. 1. 36)

101

A Dragon

Frotho's father, Hadding, had depleted the treasury with military campaigns and did not have the means to pay his army. As he was diligently looking for necessary supplies, he was inspired by the singing of an approaching local:

An island lies not far away in whose gently sloping hills
lurks a wealth of plunder.
The hill's owner who keeps this exceptional hoard
is a serpent twisted intricately in numerous curls
 drawing the winding circles of its tail
brandishing the many spirals and spitting venom.
To win you need to cover your shield with a bull hide
 and you need to protect your body with cowhide.
This will keep the bitter poison which it spews
from searing your naked limbs.
Maintain your mind's habit of bravery
 and do not be afraid of the triple forked tongue that springs forth vibrating,
from the gaping mouth.
Likewise do not fear its spiky teeth or its strength.
And do not fear the severity of the jabs
that issue rapidly from its throat.
Its strong scales do not fear weapons,
but I know the right place to stick your iron.
With the tip of your sword, search out
and find the middle of the snake's belly.
Then you can safely go to the hill with a pick-ax.
You can examine and dig through the caves.
Soon your moneybags will be crammed with wealth
and then you can drive your loaded ship back to the coast. [398]

Monster Fight

Swanwhite saw that Thorila's teenage stepsons were surrounded by phantasms while on night watch over their herd. The sisters wanted to dismount, but Swanwhite stopped them with the sound of this poem.

I see the monsters running and jumping,
hurling their bodies into night places.
The demon is waging war, given over to a dangerous brawl
he fights violently in the middle of the dangerous turmoil.
These phantasms brought images frightful to the spectators.
The land would not allow any humans to endure it.
The army rushing precipitously through the vacant air
orders us to stop and remain seated
and to turn our reigns and get out of these sacred fields.
They forbid us to go further in these lands.

---

[398] (1. 1. 38)

A menacing chorus of ghosts rose up, running headlong through the air
and issued vast sounds to the stars.
A throng of Fauns, Pans and Satyrs came
and mixed in with the monsters to fight ferociously
with fierce expressions.
Eagles and dangerous demons and witches are eager
to share the road.
The Furies are poised in a jump and
ghosts and ape devils were gathered together with them.
Terror comes trampling the road underfoot.
Staying on our tall horses' backs makes us more secure.[399]

Thor's Might

Regner therefore had no fear of any monstrous powers other than that of Thor as the magnitude of Thor's strength is not equaled by any other—human or divine. Such black and blue filth of terrible ghosts should not intimidate a manly heart. They maintain the transitory condition of their bodies by drawing from the delicate air. Their visages are endowed with a counterfeit pallor. . . .

Swanhild remained battling an obscene throng of monsters that night. In the dawn she recognized on the land the shapes of various ghosts and bizarre looking phantoms. She saw among these the likeness of Thorhild herself riddled with numerous wounds.[400]

Bring your eyes closer and peer through my arms
First sanctify your eyes with the victory symbol
for the power to safely know the imminence of Mars.

The Biarki said:
If I am able to look upon Frigg's spouse
however much he is sheltered by his white shield
and turns his tall horse,
he will not leave Lethra unphased.
Rightly is the war god struck down in combat.[401]

Loyalty Oaths

At that time, those about to become a king's retainer customarily swore fealty by touching the sword's hilt.[402]

Forest Ladies Decide Battles

Hother was hunting at that time. He was led from his path and into a fog where he interrupted a conclave of forest maidens. They greeted him calling his name. He

---

[399] II (1. 1. 38)
[400] (1. 1. 44)
[401] (1. 1. 66)
[402] (1. 1. 67)

asked them who they were. They told him that they governed wars and their outcomes by their auspices and by their commands. They are often present in wars though no one can see them. With their clandestine aid they help their chosen triumph. They said they could inflict defeat or grant victory at their will.

Balder

They also told him that Balder was set ablaze when he saw his foster sister, Nanna, bathing. They warned him not to hack Balder with weapons, even if he deserved infinite hatred. Balder is semi-divine, conceived by arcane seed in heaven, they said. After receiving this news, he suddenly saw that the lodging had disappeared and that he was exposed and abandoned without shelter in the middle of a field under a cloudless sky. He was amazed at the illusory building, the truly unusual and swift disappearance of the maidens, and the alteration of the location. But he did not realize what was going on around him, that it was all a such a joke, an empty illusion fabricated by magic tricks. . . .

The Satyr Miming and a Sword

The holy strength of Balder's physique would not yield to iron. But Gevarus added that he knew of a sword that was warded by an extremely tightly shut gate. Miming, a wood satyr, owned it. He also owned an armband with an amazing secret virtue; it would make its owner richer. But the trackless entrances to these places were full of obstructions and not at all readily accessible to mortals.[403]

That is how he was going to be able to get the sword and the armband. One of these was good for wealth, the other for war. Either one would be a huge prize for its owner. . . .

During a night watch his mind wandered, stunned by its cares. By chance he saw the satyr's shadow on his tent and he tried for it with his spear. He struck the satyr and dropped him. He roped the satyr to keep him from getting away. Then he viciously made the most dire threats against the satyr demanding the sword and the armband. The satyr did not hesitate to purchase his security and he brought out what Gevarus sought. [404]

Nanna Gives Balder a Rain-Check

While this was going on in Halogaland, Balder went armed into Gavari's borders to demand the beautiful Nanna. He was told to go find out how Nanna's mind was disposed to this. Balder approached the girl with exquisite verbal allurements. But he was getting nowhere with her. He insisted that she tell him why. She told him that a marriage between a mortal and a god could not work because the huge difference in their natures would keep them from fornicating together. Not only that, but gods sometimes breach their contracts; sometimes they suddenly sunder the contractual bonds binding them to lesser folks. The bonds between such different sorts are not stable; the fortunes of the humble always suffer among the lofty. Besides this, wealth and poverty do not share the same tent. Nor is there a firm legal right of society between splendid wealth and obscure poverty. The divine is not yoked to the earthly. Their discordant heritages,

---

[403] (1. 1. 70)
[404] (1. 1. 71)

and the nature of things, create such a gulf that the infinite majesty of the bright gods is too far from human mortality. . . .

Gods in Battle

The fleet fought hand to hand with Balder. You would have believed that gods were battling with men. Odin and Thor were fighting along with Balder in the sacred army of gods.

You would have seen human and godly might mixed in battle. But Hother was equipped with an iron resistant tunic. He broke the Gods' most densely packed wedge formations. He pressed against them as much as the terrestrial can against the heavenly. With a well-aimed cudgel shot, Thor mangled the obstacle presented by all their shields together. He was inviting the attacking hostiles to have at him as much as he was defending his allies. No kind of arm stood up against Thor's smiting. No one could safely receive his shots. Whatever he struck, he ruined. Neither shield not helmet withstood the impact of his oak. Neither magnitude of body, nor strength, offered protection. The Gods would have won, but Hother, after his battle lines were driven back, advanced swiftly and rendered Thor's mace useless by cutting it off at the handle. The gods suddenly fled when they lost that weapon.[405]

Balder saved himself by running away. Though the victors had beaten the gods, whose ships they had hacked and sunk with their, that was not enough for them; they had to savagely hack up the rest of the fleet to gratify their murderous desire for war. . . .

Fro in Uppsala

Fro established his chair not far from Uppsala, the gods' seat of government. There he changed a venerable and successful sacrificial custom practiced by the whole folk throughout the ages into a sad shocking propitiation. He began killing human victims with this disgusting libation to pay the gods. [406]

Balder

The three nymphs blended a strong potion made from the poison of three serpents into Balder's dinner. . . . Those same nymphs kindly and compassionately gave him a meticulously crafted shining and powerful victory belt. Proserpina showed herself to Hother the next night in a dream. Standing before him, she announced that he would enjoy her embrace in three days. This was no empty dream. . . .

Gave Robbing

Harold was the leader of a war band in our own times. The grave mound's fame was thriving and Harold undertook to plunder the grave at night in the hope of getting rich. Sudden horror terminated their project. The mountain top was seen too break apart and suddenly and a powerful torrent of roaring water burst forth. A swiftly rushing wall of water hurtled down and swept over the camp engulfing anything in its way. The diggers were stricken down at the water's onslaught. They threw down their pick-axes

---

[405] (1. 1. 72)
[406] (1. 1. 74)

and ran away in the chaos. They thought that they would be swept up in the rushing vortices if they did not abandon the project. Thus the gods warding that place struck sudden terror into the minds of the young men and converted their thoughts from greed to safety. They taught them to be eager to live and made them abandon their greedy undertaking. This spring was some kind of illusion created by magic and did not really come from the earth's deep innards.[407]

Shape Changing

Skilled magicians could, at one time, change their features instantly and go about in various guises. They were not only skilled in imitating the bodily appearances of people of whatever age, but they could imitate their bearing as well. . . .

Songs Carved on Bark

Odin touched her with a piece of bark marked with songs and she became like a mad woman. This was a modest vengeance to inflict for the kind of continual injuries she had dealt him. [408]

Songs Carved on a Bone

The story has it that Ollerus was such an artful magician that he could cross the sea on a bone inscribed with dire songs instead of using a boat. He overcame the challenge of the waves as swiftly as if propelled by oars.

Odin Returns

But Odin had gotten back the insignia of his divinity and he shone over the whole world with such a bright reputation, that everyone greeted him as if he were a light coming back to the world. There was not a spot on the globe that did not acknowledge the power of his divinity.

Rind and Bo

When Odin found that his son by Rind, Bo, was eager for the labors of the battlefield, he called for him and bade him to remember his brother's disaster. It would be better to exact vengeance on his brother's killers than to oppress harmless people. It is more suitable and wholesome to meet in war when the just license of revenge makes war a pious thing. . . . After that, Hother summoned the nobles to council. He told them that he was going to war against Bo and that he was going to die. He said there was not a mere doubtful conjecture, but was the credible prediction of a skilled diviners.[409]

Ubbi

Ubbi had a strong body and was great with incantations.[410]

---

[407] (1. 1. 75)
[408] (1. 1. 79)
[409] (1. 1. 81)
[410] (1. 1. 85)

Amlet and Funerary Suicide
Hermeturde professed a virile faithfulness to her husband, Amlet, and pledged that she would not desert him even in the battle line. She was disgusted by women who were afraid to follow their husbands to their graves.[411]

Fridleif's Steel Proof Shirt
Besides an innate strength of mind, Fridleif wore a steel proof shirt.   . . . Gunholm customarily dulled enemy blades with her songs. Fridleif battered his head repeatedly and drove the life out of him.[412]

Storm bringing at Sea
Oddo took in Hrafn, whom the Danes at that time regarded as the greatest pirate. Oddo knew magic. He roamed around in a boat on the deep and would capsize hostile vessels by raising violent storms with his songs. Therefore he refused to descend into contests of naval strength with pirates. He usually smashed their ships by driving terrible waves into them. . . . As the battle with the North men started, he dimmed the enemies' eyes with powerful songs such that the distracted Danes thought that the far away swords the Danes had drawn were flickering with flames and casting off rays. Their sight was so dulled that they could not look at steel drawn from its scabbard. Their vanquished eyes were unable to endure the bright illusory flashing.[413]

Three Serpents on a String
He saw three serpents suspended overhead by a string. Foul drool rolled from their gaping mouths and was to be incorporated into the recipe. Two dark black snakes hung there above them and a third whose scales were pale hung along with them. The pale snake was hung by a knot around its tail, while the black snakes had strings tied around their abdomens. . . .

A Ceremonial Meal Gives Power
Eric was revitalized by the well boding ceremonial meal. He crossed over into the summit of human knowledge by this private working. He could hardly believe the potency of this food, for it had endowed him with a knowledge of all the sciences and even allowed him to understand the talk of both wild and domestic animals. He became exceptionally skilled not only in the humanities, but also understood animal emotions. He knew their moods by their sounds. He also became eloquent and his speech became polite and ornate, such that whenever he wanted to talk, he could polish his speech with a stream of charming proverbs.

When Kraka found out that the servings had been switched so that Erik had gotten the more potent portion, she was sorely grieved; the fortune she had readied for her son went to her stepson. Soon she was groaning and began to entreat Erik never to abandon his brother now that his mother had given him such a treasure trove of unusual blessings. Indeed, it seemed that by eating a single delicious dinner, he had attained the height of

---

[411] IV (1.1. 106)
[412]

[413]

107

eloquence and reason, plus the ability to constantly win fights. She went on to say that Roller had gained a nearly equal capacity for council and that he would partake of some of the destiny she had intended for him. She also warned them that if extreme violence makes it necessary, they could call her name and she would quickly help out since godly might dwelled within her. She said she could rely on Godly power as if she was a god's associate.[414]

Favorable Interpretation of a Bad Omen

Erik reached the port that was close to where Frothi stayed. He unexpectedly stumbled and fell to the ground as his foot left the boat. He saw this fall as a good omen and divined that this lame start would be the beginning of better things.[415]

A Niding Pole

Having gotten what he demanded, Grep set out for the coast with a handpicked throng of magicians. The first thing he did therefore was to sacrifice a horse to the gods. He cut off its head and set it on a stake. He set sticks in its mouth to hold it wide open. He hoped this atrocious sight would terrify Eric and frustrate his first attempts. Grep truly believed that the barbarians' inept minds would be horrified by sight of the decapitated head.

Erik was on his way to them when he saw it. He looked at the head from afar and realized that it was an instrument of evil and ordered his companions to be silent and cautious and that none thoughtlessly utter any hasty words. Otherwise their reckless speech would leave them open to witchcraft; if there were any need for words, he would speak for everyone. They were separated by a river. They had fixed the stake with the horse head on the shore nearest themselves to discourage Erik from crossing the bridge.

Dauntless, Erik strode towards the bridge. On the other side he spoke: "May their luck load diminish and may our fortunes get better. Let bad things fall upon the wicked. May this unlucky burden's weight bury its bearer. My stronger omens bestow luck upon us!" Nor did things turn out otherwise than as he had hoped. Suddenly the neck shook loose and the head was thrown down. The stake crashed down on its bearer. Thus did the equipment of all these evil-doers expire and become worthless for what they hoped for; all at the order of a single curse.[416]

They had just learned from the Frothi's incident how the Gods had helped them out in very tough scrapes and defended them for being upright. Should they remain upright, he told them, they could expect similar help in future difficulties.[417]

As the swords menaced his head in the insidious attack, he was justified in testing that needful remedy; he called his step-mother by name during this danger as she had told him to do.[418]

---

[414] (1. c, 129 s.)
[415] (1. 1. 132)
[416] (1. 1. 134)
[417] (1. 1. 145)

The first fight would be an omen of the future since successes at the start of wars generally augur well for the future.[419]

Ship Burials

Frothi gathered together the peoples he had subdued and issued a law that whenever the head of a household should die in battle he should be buried in a grave hill with his all his arms and his horse. . . . He established that a centurion or satrap should be burned in his own ship. A king or war leader would be burned in his own ship, but one boat would serve for the incineration of ten helmsmen.[420]

Grave Robbery and a Ghoul

A disease struck down Aswith and it was ordered that he be buried in a cave in the earth with his dog and his horse. Asmund allowed himself to be entombed alive along with Aswith. They left food for him to feast on. Now Eric and his army had traveled over the heights and happened upon Aswith's tomb. The Swedes thought it held a treasure hoard so they hacked into it with pick axes. They discovered the cave was far deeper than they had expected. To negotiate it, one of them had to be let down into it on a rope. One of the readiest young men was chosen by lot for this job.

When Asmund saw the young man coming down in a wicker basket on a rope, he straight away dumped him out. Asmund climbed into the basket himself and signaled for the rope handlers standing above to bring him up. They hauled the basket up hoping for wealth. But when they noticed this strange shape, they were terrified by its unusual appearance. They thought it was a dead man who came back to life. They threw down their ropes and ran. Asmund looked awful, indeed. His horrible face looked just like it was covered with funerary rot.

Asmund began yelling loudly that he was alive and their fears needless, trying to call back the fleeing men. When Erik saw him, he was amazed at the sight of the blood running down his gory face. Aswith had been coming back to life in the night. During one of their many fights, Aswith tore off Asmund's left ear. This left a bleeding scar on his foul and chaotic face. The people standing around asked how he had gotten this wound and he told them this:

What is so amazing about my color leaving me?
A living man naturally fades when among the dead.
All the world's houses are severe to the lonely.
Miserable are those luck has left deprived of human support.
This old cave, the darkness and the numbing night
have ripped joy from my eyes and spirit.
. . .
Besides all that, I had to fight against a lifeless force

418

[419] (1. 1. 151)
[420] (1. 1. 156)

and against monstrous danger and terrible stress.
Back from death, Aswith rushed at me, clawing me with his nails;
after death he waged a terrible war.
What is so amazing about my color leaving me?
A living man naturally fades when among the dead.
I do not know what divine Stygian enterprise
Aswith's spirit was sent from the lower world to undertake.
He devoured his swift footed horse with savage teeth,
he even offered his dog to his ghastly jaws.
Not contented with eating his horse and his dog,
he brought his swift nails against me,
gashing my cheek and taking my ear.
Hence the shocking appearance of my torn face,
gore issues from the savage wound.
But that monster hardly escaped unpunished.
I cut his head off with my iron
I pierced his criminal body with a stake.

What is so amazing about my color leaving me?
A living man naturally fades when among the dead.[421]

Shape Shifting

Among them there was a matron skilled in magic who put more hope in her art than she had fear of the savage king. She roused in her son a desire to secretly steal the king's hoard. She promised that he would get away with it. She told him that Frothi stood at the edge of death and carried his senile mind around in the remains of a sick body. When he warned his mother of the magnitude of the danger, she told him to hope for better. She said that an expecting sea-cow or something similar would prevent Frothi's vengeance. Her voice quieted his fears, and drove him to do her bidding.

When this was done, it was as if Frothi had been torn by an affront. He violently attacked and laid waste to her house. Men were sent to seize her and her children and bring them before him. But the woman had foreknowledge of this. She deceived her enemies with magic by shape-shifting into the form of a mare. Upon Frothi's arrival, she transformed her appearance to that of a sea-cow and seemed to be wandering along the shore in search of food. To her sons she gave the shape of foals with smaller bodies. The king was captivated by wonder at these monsters. He ordered that they be surrounded to block their way back to the sea.

The King

Finally, the king got down from the wagon he needed to carry his weak and aged body. He sat down on the ground and marveled at the creatures. But the mother, who had assumed the shape of a larger beast, aimed her horn and attacked the king, stabbing him in the side. The wound killed him; such an unworthy exit for such a majestic man.

---

[421] (1. 1. 160)

110

His soldiers wanted vengeance for his death and pierced the monsters with their spears. Once they had killed these monsters, the soldiers discovered the bodies of humans with the heads of beasts. This showed them the greatness of the magic.

Embalming the King's Corpse
After he died, Frothi was one of the world's most famous kings. They gutted him, cured his body with salt, and looked after it for three years.[422]

Swan's Song
Fridlief left the camp at night to scout. He heard a strange percussive sound in the air nearby. He gazed upward and his ear caught the screaming song of three swans flying overhead.

While Hythin turns the seas he cuts the swift tides
his slave drinks from gold and licks milk from cups.
The best situation for a slave is when a king
agrees to make him an heir and
and recklessly mingles their fates.

Finally, after these voices, a belt fell from the sky and it bore letters explaining the song.[423]

Three Prophetic Nymphs in a Temple
It had been a tradition since antiquity to seek an oracle from the fates regarding children's futures. In such a rite, Fridleif was about to look into his son Olaf's future. He swore serious oaths and went praying up to the goddesses' shrine. When he looked into the temple he saw that three seats were occupied by three nymphs. The first leniently granted him good looks and a plentiful abundance of popularity. The second made him big-hearted. The third woman was envious and peevish. She disdained her sisters' agreed generosity and wanted to weaken their gifts. She affixed the crime of miserliness into the boy's future nature.[424]

Thor Rips Out Starkad's Extra Arms
They say that Starkad's descent from giants was shown by his numerous outrageous hands. They say that the God Thor ripped the muscles joining four of these extra limbs and tore these abominations of nature out of him. He ripped the prodigious clump of digits from his body so that he was left with two limbs. Before this, his huge frame was thronging with appendages, but afterwards, his body was made right with a form limited by more human dimensions.[425]

---

[422] (1. 1. 170)
[423] (1. 1. 178)
[424] (1. 1. 181)
[425] (1. 1. 183)

Thor & Odin

Once there were certain people initiated in the art of sorcery. Thor and Odin, of course, were experienced in generating various amazing deceptions by which they captivated simple minds. Thus they arrogated to themselves the rank of divinities. The Norwegians, Swedes and Danes were entangled in the snares of these empty beliefs. They defiled themselves with the contagion of this peculiar deception and excited eagerness for this worship. Their fallacy's effects spread to such an extent that certain others worshipped them as if they were divine: as if they were gods or the gods' associates. They made solemn vows to these magicians and showed respect for this sacrilegious error that they should have shown to the sacred.

Holidays

It therefore came about that they believed that their series of holidays are rightly named after these gods. They knew that the Romans had named the holidays after their own gods or after the seven planets. [426]

Hanging a King

The ancients tell us that the fore-mentioned Starkad dedicated his first deeds to the Gods' favor by killing the Norwegian king, Wikar. Some have given the following account of the affair. Odin wanted Wikar dead, but did not want to do it in the open. Starkad was conspicuous because he was so uncommonly large. He was known not only for his stout heart, but also for his skill in songs. These skills could readily be employed in the king's destruction. . . .

Savage and long lasting storms vexed them. The winds kept them from sailing such that they had to spend most of the year in idleness. This led them to propitiate the Gods with human victims. Lots thrown into an urn required that they sacrifice a king. Starkad made a noose out of osier twigs and wrapped it around the king's neck, as if he was about to give only a brief illusion of an actual sacrifice. But the severe knot did its job; it hung Wikar high and tore away his breath. Starkad's steel snatched away the remains of Wikar's palpitating spirit. Starkad revealed his perfidy at that moment when he ought to have helped the king. [427]

Starkad in Uppsala

He spent seven years in Sweden with Fro's sons, and then left to associate with the Danish tyrant, Haki. He had been in Uppsala during its sacrificial time, and disdained the pansy body motions, the theatrics and clapping of actors, and the light clattering of small bells. [428]

A Premonition

(1. 1. 206)Starkad is said to sung this song: . . .

When I recently departed from you,

---

[426] (1. 1. 183)
[427] (1. 1. 184)
[428] (1. 1. 185)

My foreknowing mind found out
that you will soon die by hostile arms
You, the greatest king.

When I was wayfaring
in a distant countryside,
a prescient groan arose in my mind
indicating that I would not see you again.[429]

Soul-Catching

Only Frothi refused to believe that Harald's sons were dead. He sought out their hiding place with a skilled seeress. Her songs were so powerful that she seemed to be able to call things to her touch, including distant things that were visible only to her, even if they were bound fast in knots. She told him that a certain Regni was secretly raising them and had given them dog names for the purpose of hiding them.

When they found themselves being pulled from their hideout by the strange violence of the songs and that they were being dragged into the seeress's sight, they showered her lap with their guardians' gold to keep from being brought out under such forceful and terrible coercion. After she got the money, she suddenly fell as if dying, acting like she was sick. Her attendants asked why she had suddenly collapsed and she told them that it was impossible to find out where Harald's sons were hiding because they had special powers to resist even the fiercest songs.[430]

Iron Nails

He found out that Erik's warrior, Hakon, was skilled in dulling blades with songs, so he fixed iron nails into a great wooden mace for bludgeoning.[431]

Libations

The Swedes started to think that Haldan was the son of the powerful Thor, and the people gave him sacred honors and deemed him worthy of libations.[432]

Whatever order the foreknowing fates tie together,
whatever secrets of divine reason they may draft
whatever foreseen series of future events they hold,
no alteration of our frail affairs can stop.[433]

Infertility Cured By Honoring a Dead Relative

Haldan found out that Gyuritha was barren, but he desperately wanted children, so he went to Uppsala to get a remedy for her infertility. The oracular prophesy warned that

---

[429] (1. 1. 185)
[430] VII (1. 1. 217)
[431] (1. 1. 219)
[432] (1. 1. 220)
[433] (1. 1. 243)

he needed to hold a memorial service for his brother's spirit if he wanted children. Indeed, he did sire a child by Gyuritha, and named him Harald.[434]

Harald had an exceptional physique and was really big; he was bigger and taller than other folks of his era. He had known Odin's indulgence, and seems to have been born to Odin's oracle. Steel could not harm him. Weapons that would wound others could not wound Starkad. This favor did not go unrewarded. He promised Odin all the souls driven from their bodies by his steel.[435]

Odin Teaches Harald Some Tactics

Harald wanted to have oracles look into the matter further. An extraordinarily large old one-eyed man appeared to him. He was covered in a furry mantle and told Harald he was known as Odin and that he was experienced in the art of war. He offered up to Harald an exceedingly useful plan for organizing his army into battle formation.[436]

Odin Disguised

Odin, disguised by his name and his style of dress undertook an insidious mission to dissolve the king's close friendship.[437]

Odin Withholds Victory

Bruni's silence made the king realize that this was Odin. This numinous entity, once like family to him, was now in his presence in an altered appearance, either to give or withhold help. He was soon pleading with all his might for the Danes to win one last battle, since he had been kind toward them before. He promised Odin that he would equal the original gift by giving him the souls of the fallen.[438]

King Consigned to Flames in a Ship

Ring thought that they needed to hold a memorial service for Harald's ghost. After they found Harald's body and his cudgel, Ring dedicated, in Harald's honor, his own steed, upon which he mounted a fine golden saddle, and joined it to his royal wain. Ring then swore grave oaths and prayed that Harald, this mount's rider, might precede his comrades in death to Tartarus, and that he might there intercede with Pluto, the underworld's guardian and ask that he make this place pleasant for friends and foes alike.

Ring erected a pyre and ordered the Danes to pile their king's golden boat onto the fire. With the king's body cast onto the fire and burning, Ring began making rounds among the grieving nobles, and rather immoderately began pressuring them to liberally give as fuel to the fire, arms, gold, or whatever valuables they had. He said they would all thereby send it all over to the veneration of a worthy king. After the king's corpse had

---

[434] (1. 1. 246)
[435] (1. 1. 247)
[436] (1. 1. 248)
[437] (1. 1. 255)
438

114

been completely consumed, he had ashes put in an urn and had the urn taken to Leire to be buried with the king's steed and weapons in accordance with royal custom.[439]

Starkad Dies

Starkad eagerly offered his sword to Hather and leaned his head forward. He encouraged Hathar not to wield the iron like a woman or to do the job timidly. Starkad also told Hathar that he would become impervious to weapons if, right after the decapitation, but before the body fell, he would go between the head and the body. It is hard to say whether Starkad said this to teach or to punish his slayer. The extraordinary mass of Starkad's cadaver might have crushed him as he jumped. Hathar therefore energetically hacked the old man's head with his sword. When the severed head hit the dirt it bit the ground; the savagery of its death bite showed the ferocity of Starkad's spirit. The killer did not make the reckless jump as he thought that the truth was hidden in a false promise.[440]

Lots for Exile

Lots for each were cast into an urn and those whose lots were drawn were declared exiles.[441]

Gorm Seeks after the Mysteries

Gorm had acquired his father's adventurousness, but he expressed it differently; instead of using weapons, he delved into the wonders of nature. While other kings' sons were mad with war-lust, Gorm was deeply inspired to seek out wonders. He sought knowledge through tales and personal experience. He had a penchant for looking into the unusual and the extraordinary. Gorm therefore gave the highest priority to checking an Icelandic tale about a certain Geruth's dwelling place.[442]

Holy Cows

One monster was much larger than the others. He bore a huge cudgel and strode out into the ocean. He hollered at them as he drew near, telling them that they could not sail away unless they paid for cattle they had killed. The price for the reduced herd of holy cows was to be one man from each ship. Thorkil succumbed to this menace and handed over three men chosen by lot. . . .

In the Giant Home

Thorkil ordered his retinue not to speak with any who might catch up with them. Thorkil told them that he was the only one among them who had experience in giant ways and traditions. As such he was the only one who could talk to giants without danger, he added. He warned them that giants' greatest power against strangers came from the strangers' rude talk.[443]

---

[439] (1. 1. 264)
[440] (1. 1. 273 s)
[441] (1. 1. 284)
[442]
[443] (1. 1. 287)

Golden Bridge to the Other World

As they journeyed they saw a golden bridge over a river. The retinue wanted to cross it, but Guthmund ordered them back and told them that this river was the border between the world of mortals and the supernatural world and that crossing was forbidden to humans.[444]

Thor Was There

As they approached they saw broken chunks of a cliff. An old man with a pierced body sat nearby on a scaffolding across from the fragmented cliff. Three weak old women with bad backs and tumor-ridden bodies reclined on beds right next to each other. Thorkil was versed in the underlying causes of things and instructed his inquisitive associates on this matter. He said that the God Thor had been offended by the giants' arrogance and hurled a hot piece of steel into Geruth's midsection as Geruth was fighting against him. The steel pierced through the giant and dropped further away after striking and convulsing the cliff face. Thorkil said that Thor smote the women with a lightening blast's violence and that their broken bodies were the price they paid for assailing Thor's godhood.

Greed and Treasure

After leaving, they came to seven clay barrels girded with golden bands. The barrels were bound together by a multitude of interwoven silver rings. Next to these they discovered a strange beast's gold tipped tooth. Near this they found a huge bovine horn, finely worked, and exquisitely flashing with precious stones. An exceptionally heavy armband lay beside it. But this was not without a hidden cunning.

One man's greed flared up and he grabbed for the gold. He did not know that a pernicious doom and horrible death lurked hidden behind the metal's superb splendor. A second man lost control of greed's power; his unsteadied hands reached for the horn. A third man, following the confidence of the others, lost control of his fingers and bore the tooth on his shoulders. This plunder looked attractive, its pleasing workmanship was outstanding and exhibited an alluring aspect to the eye.

The armband changed into a serpent and its sharp venomous teeth struck at its wearer. The horn stretched out into a dragon and ripped life's breath away from its bearer. The tooth turned into a sword and immersed its point in its wearer's innards. The others wailed at the horrifying destruction of their comrades. Though they had not sinned, they were not confident that their innocence would save them.

Finally, a back door to a second chamber showed them a more narrow and isolated room, which revealed a secret room with an even richer hoard. Before them lay arms too large for the bodies of humans. They saw among these a kingly general's cloak with a fine felt cap joined to a wondrously worked weapon belt. Thorkil became captivated by wonder and threw off the reigns to his own desire. He cast off his mind's temperate intentions, and thereby instructed the others not to check their appetites. He

---

[444] (1. 1. 288)

116

laid his hands on the general's cloak, and his reckless example gave the others permission to plunder.

An unexpected concussion began to shake the inmost recesses from the deepest foundations. The women clamored that these wicked pirates had been tolerated too long. Suddenly, the shapes they had thought dead or semi-dead, jumped up from their chairs, as if the womens' clamors had directed them, and began furiously attacking the foreigners. The others began roaring raucously.

Then Buchi and Broder resorted to a tactic once familiar to them. They advanced striking the attacking lamias with arrows in all directions and crushed that monster troop by torturing it with their bows and slings. No other power could have warded off the monsters so effectively. But the bowman's art only saved twenty of the king's retinue. The monsters had shredded the others.[445]

Ugartloki
Their sailing proved rewarding at first, but then bad weather shook Thorkel until his companions were about to die of hunger. Thorkil's mind veered toward religion now that only a few companions were left and he resorted to praying to gods. He thought that for their protection in this extreme necessity they needed divine help. While some were invoking various godly powers with prayers, and agreeing to placate the sacred majesty of various heavenly powers, Gorm called on UgartLoki. He made sacrifices and swore oaths and thereby got the stretch of mild weather they had hoped for.[446]

He brought fire back to his retinue. They got a lenient wind and Thorkil entered their port of destination on the fourth day. Thorkil and his retinue went ashore into a land where night's endless presence frustrated changing light. Painfully, Thorkill's eyes got used to the darkness, and discerned an extraordinarily massive cliff. He was eager to explore that crag. When he came to an entrance he ordered his retinue to stand guard outside and to make sparks by striking stones together to keep the demons at bay.

Ugarloki's Cave
Light held by the others shone before him. Thorkil submitted his body to the cave's narrow throat. He observed that on all sides there were many rows of iron chairs among a multitude of slithering snakes. From there he saw a rather pleasant stream flowing smoothly over a gravel bed. He crossed the stream and came to point where the cave sloped gently. From there the visitors could see an obscene room. Inside appeared Ugartloki; his hands and feet were weighed down with a mass of immense chains. His stinky hairs were as big and strong as spears made of cornel wood.

Thorkil and his comrades began pulling one of these hairs from the resigned Ugartloke's chin. Thorkil wanted to have ready confirmation of their deeds. Right away a mighty stink poured out over the bystanders so they could not breathe except by covering their noses with their coats.

---

[445] (1. 1. 290)
[446] (1. 1. 292)

They had hardly gotten out when the serpents began diving at them from all sides and spitting on them. Only five of Thorkil's retinue were able to get into the ship with their leader; poison killed the rest. The savage demons menaced those who were exposed by casting down poisonous spit all over the place. The sailors held up skins to serve as umbrellas to repel the falling venom. When one of the sailors wanted to see what was going on, venom struck his head and it took it off just as if by a sword stroke. A second man was blinded when he peered out from under the umbrella. Another man was adjusting the covering when a potent chunk of rot took off his arm.

The others therefore willingly and uselessly prayed to their gods. But Thorkil made vows to the universal god. After he had poured out libations with his prayers, the weather quickly improved and combined for him clear skies and good sailing.[447]

The stinky hair, which Thorkil had yanked from the giant's head as proof of their great deeds, sprayed all over the bystanders and killed some of them.[448]

Sivard Snake-in-the-Eye Gets his Snakes

An exceedingly tall man was seen going to Sivard's bed. He said he was named Roftar. Roftar promised Sivard that his health would return as soon as he agreed to give him the spirits of those he would strike down in battle. . . . Finally, Roftar sprinkled dust into Sivard's pupils, and then left. Suddenly stains appeared in Sivard's awe struck eyes, and they looked very much like little snakes. I think this miracle's author wanted to reveal the youth's future savage temper with the conspicuous testimony of his eyes and that this discerning part of his body should remain a foreshadowing of his future. An old lady who brought his medicinal potions saw the sign of the little snakes in his eyes and was terrified by the strange lad. She fainted and fell, giving up her ghost.[449]

A Seeress

Suddenly, a small woman seeress rendered an advantageous prediction for the king, as if she were a celestial oracle, or an interpreter of divine will.[450]

A Bad Conversion

He converted to the Roman Rites, profaned the error of the perfidious, destroyed temples, proscribed sacrifices, and abolished the priesthood. He was the first to bring Christianity to his disorderly fatherland. He emulated the holy by rejecting the worship of demons.[451]

---

[447] (1. 1. 294)
[448] (1. 1. 296)
[449] IX (1. 1. 304)
[450] (1. 1. 306)
[451] (1. 1. 313)

A Sword between them in their Bed

Thyra tenaciously insisted that they not consumate their marriage until the passing of three days. In reality, she had decided not to have sex until she could have a dream to tell whether their congress would produce children. . . .

He placed a sword between himself and his bride so they would not touch each other. He also arranged the bed in two sections in a tent-like fashion.[452]

---

[452] (1. 1. 319)

W

wagon, 74
wain, 7, 10, 114
wakes, 81
walking backwards, 83
wall, 100, 105
war, 4, 8, 13, 19, 20, 24, 25, 26, 27, 31,
  36, 47, 71, 78, 79, 90, 92, 96, 97, 102,
  103, 104, 105, 106, 109, 110, 114, 115
war god, 25
warh, 89
warp, 81
Wassail
  Weasseil, 95
water, 13, 29, 34, 56, 64, 66, 70, 73, 74,
  77, 80, 83, 89, 100, 105
waters, 10, 14, 15, 19, 20, 24, 28, 32, 61,
  94
wax, 33, 83
wealth, 102, 104, 109
weapons, 7, 10, 13, 38, 42, 47, 76, 86
weave, 80, 92
weavers, 92, 93
Wechta, 65
wedge formations, 105
Wednesday, 95
wehadic, 43
werewolf, 75
west, 26, 28, 43, 63
whinnies
  whinny, 7, 71
whistling, 67
white, 4, 7, 25, 32, 71, 79, 84
wicker, 8
wife, 8, 20, 27, 32, 35, 38, 39, 40, 47,
  58, 62, 68, 92, 98, 99, 101
Wikar, 112
Willibrord, 52, 56, 67, 69

wine, 30, 73, 82, 83, 95
wings, 84
Winniles, 39, 58
winter, 28, 90, 100
wisdom, 24, 26, 78
witchcraft, 21, 22, 33, 38, 39, 45, 49, 72,
  88, 90, 108
witness, 12, 22, 42
witnesses, 21, 22, 42
wizards, 23, 54
Woden, 36, 37, 47, 65, 90, 92, 94
wolves, 101
womb of nations, 24
women's clothes, 10
wood, 8, 9, 13, 32, 37, 54, 60, 63, 76, 83,
  97, 104, 117
wood fire, 13
wooden, 30, 37, 59, 96, 113
wooden dove, 59
Wooden feet, 50
wooden foot, 59
wooden sculptures, 30
woods, 7, 9, 13, 30, 52, 63, 71, 101
woof, 81
wool, 74, 92
woolen, 80
worm, 75
worship, 6, 10, 19, 25, 26, 28, 31, 34, 40,
  46, 47, 50, 64, 67, 71, 72, 78, 80, 85,
  86, 89, 90, 94, 98, 112, 118
worshipped, 6, 7, 16, 17, 18, 25, 27, 34,
  37, 55, 56, 58, 61, 62, 63, 64, 65, 66,
  68, 78, 84, 86, 87
Wotan, 57, 90
wreaths, 4
writings, 4, 19, 36, 45

Y

yrias, 50

www.ingramcontent.com/pod-product-compliance
Lightning Source LLC
Chambersburg PA
CBHW020251290326
41930CB00039B/712